Healthier
COMFORT FOOD

Feel-good recipes
with fewer calories

DD
COOK
BOOK

'COMFORT FOOD' IS AN EMOTIVE
PHRASE – IT CONJURES UP IMAGES
OF TANTALISING, MOUTH-WATERING
DISHES THAT WARM YOU UP AND
FEED YOUR SOUL.

It's meltingly tender casseroles, flavourful take-aways, fish & chips, moreish cakes, sticky puddings and more…

Healthy eating doesn't have to mean uninspiring food, mediocre taste and going hungry. Good nutritious food, can (and is in this book!) be comforting, filling and delicious too.

Eating healthily is about giving your body a great, balanced diet, full of good-quality produce. And if it's put together well – it tastes great too!

Flick through the pages of this book and begin enjoying easy-to-prepare gorgeous healthy food at home every day.

RECIPE TESTING

Every recipe in this book has been tested three times: first by the recipe writer, then by an everyday home-cook and finally by the food stylist at the photo shoot. We ensure that all ingredients are readily available, the method makes perfect sense, and that each one is delicious.

RECIPE NOTES

Each recipe is written in a style that's easy to follow. There are preparation and cooking times, nutritional information, serving suggestions, cook's tips and space for your own notes too.

- F Suitable for freezing
- V Suitable for vegetarians (provided that suitable cheeses, yogurts etc. are used)
- V Suitable for vegans (check labels)

Nutritional information has been calculated by portion or item. Where there are portion variations, e.g. serves 6–8, the analysis given is based on the larger number. Sugar is 'free sugars' (added sugars, including those naturally present in fruit juice and syrups).

Spoon measures are level unless otherwise stated.

Eggs are large unless otherwise stated in the ingredients.

SAFETY NOTES

Recipes using nuts or nut products are not suitable for young children or those with a nut allergy. Certain at-risk groups, such as pregnant women, babies and sick or elderly people, should not eat raw or lightly cooked eggs.

A WELL-BALANCED DIET

Nutrition is a very complex area, however there are a few simple guidelines that most of us can follow to help us on our way to a healthy diet.

1 Eat plenty of veg

Delicious, packed full of fibre and a whole host of vital nutrients. Fill at least a third, or even half of your plate with vegetables: raw, steamed, roast, mashed, stir-fried – however you like them!

2 Add colour!

Aim to make your meals as colourful as possible. Different coloured vegetables and fruit contain numerous nutrients and eating the rainbow helps you to consume a variety of vitamins and minerals. See the image below for further info on getting your 5 (or more) a day.

RED
Tomato	1
Cherry tomatoes	7
Rhubarb (cooked)	2 tbsp
Strawberries	7
Cherries	14
Pepper	½

ORANGE
Orange	1
Nectarine	1
Apricots	3
Carrots	3 tbsp
Baked beans	3 tbsp
Sweet potato	1

YELLOW
Banana	1
Grapefruit	½
Pineapple	1 slice
Sweetcorn	3 tbsp
Yellow lentils	3 tbsp
Chickpeas	3 tbsp

GREEN
Apple	1
Melon	1 slice
Lettuce	1 bowl
Peas	3 tbsp
Green beans	4 tbsp
Avocado	½

PURPLE
Plums	2
Blackcurrants	4 tbsp
Sultanas	1 tbsp
Kidney beans	3 tbsp
Beetroot	7 slices
Aubergine	½

WHITE
Leek	1
Cauliflower	8 florets
Mushrooms (chopped)	3 tbsp
Turnip/swede	3 tbsp
Butter beans	3 tbsp
Parsnip	1

What counts?

Almost all fruits and vegetables count towards your 5 a day. This includes fresh produce, frozen, tinned and preserved fruits and vegetables

One portion of your 5 a day…

= 80g of fruit
= 80g of vegetables
= 30g dried fruit

3 Swap white for brown

Carbohydrates are vital for energy and wholegrain (complex) carbohydrates release energy slowly and provide valuable fibre. Choose wholemeal, rye or mixed grain/seeded bread, wholewheat pasta and noodles, brown rice and keep skin on potatoes. Fill one third of your plate.

4 Eat good quality protein

Our bodies require protein for growth and repair of muscles. Choose high welfare, quality fish and meat, free-range eggs, tofu, beans, chickpeas, seeds and lentils. Fill around one-sixth of your plate (or a portion the size of your palm). Nuts and cheese are also great sources of protein, but they are calorie-dense so choose a matchbox-size portion.

5 Dairy

Dairy provides essential calcium, protein, vitamins and minerals needed for strong bones, healthy teeth and skin, for energy and to regulate metabolism. Choose milk and fat-free natural yogurt (around one-sixth of your plate or a full glass) and cheese (see 4).

6 And a little good fat

Fat is high in calories, but we still need a little in our diet as it's essential for the absorption of some vitamins and fatty acids. Opt for unsaturated fats, such as olive or rapeseed oil, oily fish, avocado or nuts.

7 Limit sugar and salt

Avoid adding unnecessary salt to your food; taste it first! And try eating as little 'free' sugar as possible. 'Free' means that it's an added sugar. Naturally occurring sugars in fruit, vegetables and milk are fine.

8 Water!

Drink plenty of water. Tap water is cheap and readily available. If you don't like the taste, invest in a water filter jug and keep it in the fridge. Keep sliced lemons or limes in your freezer, to add a little zest to your water. You can experiment with different fruits too.

These are just guidelines, based on current advice. If you have any health conditions you should seek nutritional advice from your doctor or dietitian.

PORTION SIZES

Check your crockery

Everything in moderation is a good adage. If you think that your portion sizes may be too large look at the size of your plates and bowls. You'll be tempted to fill them, which means you could be over-eating. Seek out vintage crockery – it's often smaller and useful for keeping track of your portion sizes (and can be really pretty too!)

Enjoy your food!

Sit at the table and savour each mouthful. See mealtime as a pleasure to be enjoyed for its own merits rather than a necessity.

Don't feel guilty

Don't worry if you have an indulgent day – we all love a visit to the fish & chip shop, a pub meal or slice of cake with friends. If you aim for healthy eating 80 per cent of the time that's great; don't fret about the occasional treat.

And, of course, to further boost your physical and mental wellbeing, get plenty of fresh air and exercise. Even a 20-minute brisk walk can do wonders for your health!

These are just guidelines, based on current advice. If you have any health conditions you should seek nutritional advice from your doctor or dietitian.

FILL YOUR KITCHEN WITH GOODIES

If you have healthy, nutritious ingredients in your kitchen, you're far more likely to eat a balanced diet and avoid highly processed food with added salt and sugars. Here, we have given some suggestions; tweak according to your own likes/dislikes.

Fridge

Filtered water

Fresh fruit, vegetables and salad

Fat-free natural yogurt, buttermilk, reduced fat fromage frais or crème fraîche

Milk

Cheese

Eggs

Fish and good quality lean meat or meat substitute such as tofu

Light mayonnaise, sweet chilli sauce, ketchup, mustard, horseradish, redcurrant jelly, tamarind paste, fish sauce, Turkish pepper paste, gochujang paste, hoisin sauce

Olives, artichokes and capers

Freezer

Sliced lemons/limes to liven up your drinking water

Ready-chopped: garlic, chilli, ginger, herbs, onions

Peas and sweetcorn

Batch-cooked food

Storecupboard

Fresh fruit and vegetables that don't need refrigerating

Wholemeal, seeded or rye bread, tortillas, flatbreads or sandwich thins

Poppadoms, Panko breadcrumbs

Pasta, noodles, quinoa/couscous, polenta and rice

Beans, pulses and lentils; canned or dried

Chopped tomatoes, tomato purée, passata

Canned tuna and/or salmon

All your favourite dried spices and/or herbs

Soy sauce, olive oil, rapeseed oil, sesame oil, vinegars, tabasco

Nut butter

Stock cubes, reduced fat coconut milk or creamed coconut

Nuts and seeds

Dried fruit

Oats, cornflour, dried yeast, baking powder, cocoa powder and flour

Gelatine leaves, vanilla extract

Popping corn

Honey, maple carob syrup and unrefined sugar

Garden

Herbs, fruit and veg, if you have the time (and inclination) to grow them

QUICK & EASY IDEAS

This book is packed with simple and easy recipes, but if you are very short on time, or need a little inspiration for breakfast, take a look at these speedy ideas.

Breakfast Ideas

Toasted sourdough topped with mashed avocado & poached egg – add a sprinkling of chilli flakes for a delicious kick

Porridge oats cooked in milk and topped with berries and a drizzle of honey

Natural yogurt with chopped banana, and a sprinkle of sesame or chia seeds

Homemade muesli: oats mixed with your favourite dried fruit and nuts, with milk

Rye or seeded toast with smoked salmon and soft cheese or scrambled egg

Lunch Ideas

Baked potato with beans or tuna mixed with sweetcorn and a little light mayo

Homemade soup: cook any veg left in the fridge with some lentils and stock

Wholemeal tortilla wrap with salad, griddled halloumi and sweet chilli sauce

Soy sauce mixed with a little rice wine vinegar, tossed into any salad or chopped raw veg with chickpeas and/or sliced chicken

Canned sweetcorn, chopped tomatoes and cucumber (and a few chopped herbs if you like) stirred into microwave brown basmati rice and topped with thinly sliced ham

A two-egg omelette filled with mushrooms

Seeded bread sandwich filled with grilled bacon (snip off the fat), lettuce and tomato and a smidge of light mayonnaise

Snack Ideas

Ham slices filled with coleslaw (see recipe below)

Hummus, beetroot dip or tzatziki (see recipes below) with carrot, cucumber and pepper batons

Hard boiled eggs, sliced in half with a dip of 1 tbsp light mayo mixed with a little Dijon mustard

Mix beaten eggs with cottage cheese, canned sweetcorn and a little finely chopped chorizo. Bake in muffin tins until set

A couple of Scottish oatcakes with one slice of cheese

Fresh fruit

Apple slices spread with a little nut butter

A matchbox-sized portion of nuts and/or dried fruit

Four small squares of dark chocolate

Homemade popcorn

Coleslaw

Finely shred red or white cabbage, mix with finely chopped apple, or carrot and spring onion and a mixture of light mayonnaise and reduced fat crème fraiche.

Hummus

In a food processor, whizz a can of chickpeas with 2 tbsp fat-free natural yogurt, 1 tsp tahini, 1 clove of garlic, seasoning and 2 tbsp lemon juice.

Beetroot Dip

In a food processor, whizz a pack of cooked beetroot (not in vinegar) with 75g (3oz) canned cannellini beans, 50g (2oz) feta, 5 tbsp reduced fat crème fraîche and a pinch of chilli flakes.

Tzatziki

Mix fat-free natural yogurt with finely chopped cucumber and mint.

HEARTY LUNCHES

SMOKY CARROT SOUP WITH QUINOA & FETA

Serves 4   Preparation 10 minutes   Cooking 30 minutes

Vegetable oil 1 tbsp

Onion 1 small, peeled and chopped

Ground cumin 2 tsp

Sweet smoked paprika 3 good tsp

Carrots 500g (1lb 2oz), peeled and coarsely grated

Vegetable Stock Pot 1

Three colour quinoa 50g (2oz)

Salt and freshly ground black pepper

Feta cheese 110g (4oz)

Mint leaves good handful

Balsamic vinegar

Heat the oil in a large saucepan, add the onion and spices, cover and fry gently for 5 minutes.

Add the carrots and cook, stirring occasionally, for a few minutes. Add the Stock Pot and 1 litre (1¾ pints) boiling water. Simmer, partly covered, for 20 minutes.

Meanwhile, cook the quinoa according to the pack's instructions, drain and set aside.

Using a stick blender, whizz the soup in the pan and season to taste. It should be quite thick, but add boiling water to thin it down if you prefer.

Ladle the soup into bowls, spoon a portion of quinoa in the middle and crumble feta on top. Tear the mint leaves over, then drizzle with balsamic vinegar and a grinding of black pepper.

Tip

For a spicier soup add a good pinch of chilli powder when frying the onion.

NOTES

Calories	Fibre	Salt	Sugar	Fat
180	7g	1.9g	0g	10.3g of which 4.2g is saturated

RED VELVET SOUP WITH CORN & CREAMY CHEESE

Serves 4   Preparation 30 minutes   Cooking 35 minutes

Butternut squash 275g (10oz), peeled, deseeded and cut into large chunks

Beetroot 3, halved

Tomatoes 2 large, halved

Onion 1 large, peeled and quartered

Red pepper 1, halved and deseeded

Ground cumin 1 tsp

Ground cinnamon ½ tsp

Mild chilli powder ½ tsp

Salt and freshly ground black pepper

Olive oil spray

Vegetable stock 900ml (1½ pints), hot

Tomato purée 2 tbsp

Reduced fat soft cheese 75g (3oz)

Frozen sweetcorn 4 tbsp, thawed

Snipped fresh chives 1 tbsp

Preheat the oven to 220°C/200°fan/Gas 7. Line two baking sheets with foil.

Put all the vegetables except the sweetcorn in a large bowl. Sprinkle in the cumin, cinnamon and chilli powder and season with salt and pepper. Lightly spray with olive oil and toss the vegetables to coat. Spread the vegetables over the baking sheets. Roast for 15–20 minutes until starting to soften and turn golden brown. Set aside and leave until cool enough to handle.

Rub off the beetroot skins. Tip the vegetables and any roasting juices into a large saucepan.

Add the hot stock and stir in the tomato purée. Bring to the boil then reduce the heat, cover and simmer for 15 minutes or until the vegetables are soft.

Using a stick blender, whizz until smooth, adding a little more hot stock or water to adjust the consistency if needed. Season to taste.

Blend 1–2 tablespoons cold water with the soft cheese. Ladle the soup into warmed bowls then swirl the creamy cheese into the soup and garnish with sweetcorn and fresh chives. Serve piping hot.

Tips

Use kitchen paper to protect your fingers from staining when skinning the beetroot. It will also help to grip and make it easy to peel away the beetroot skin.

Choose any combination of red and yellow vegetables, though the intense colour always requires beetroot.

Toast the corn in a dry frying pan for a nutty crunchy bite.

For a vegan soup, replace the soft cheese with a swirl of reduced fat coconut milk.

Calories	Fibre	Salt	Sugar	Fat
120	6.6g	1.4g	0g	2.1g of which 0.6g is saturated

CRAB & TARRAGON CORN CHOWDER

Serves 4   Preparation 20 minutes   Cooking 20 minutes

Olive oil 1 tsp

Fennel 1 bulb (approx. 300g/11oz), diced, reserving a few fronds to serve

Spring onions 6, trimmed and roughly chopped

Garlic 1 clove, peeled and crushed

Potatoes 200g (7oz), peeled and diced

Chopped fresh tarragon 2 tbsp, plus a few sprigs to serve

Sweetcorn 340g can, drained

Skimmed milk 300ml (½ pint)

Vegetable stock 700ml (1¼ pints)

White crab meat 2 x 145g cans, drained and flaked

Salt and freshly ground black pepper

Heat the olive oil in a large saucepan and fry the fennel, spring onions and garlic for 2–3 minutes until softened. Add the potatoes, tarragon, sweetcorn, milk and stock and bring to the boil. Cover and simmer for 10–12 minutes until the potato is soft.

Remove four ladles of the mixture and whizz in a blender until smooth. Return this mixture to the pan along with the crab meat and season to taste. Heat through, gently stirring, for 2–3 minutes or until ready to serve.

Ladle into bowls and sprinkle with tarragon sprigs and fennel fronds.

Tip

To add crunch, sprinkle some lightly crushed sea salted crackers over the chowder just before serving.

NOTES

Calories	Fibre	Salt	Sugar	Fat
225	6g	1.8g	0g	4.9g of which 0.7g is saturated

ROAST CHICKEN SOUP WITH SAGE & ONION CRUMBS

Serves 4   Preparation 20 minutes   Cooking 20 minutes

Olive oil 1 tbsp, plus spray

Onion 1, peeled and finely chopped

Celery 2 sticks, chopped

Leek 1 large, trimmed and chopped

Potatoes 250g (9oz), peeled and diced

Garlic 1 clove, peeled and crushed

Rosemary 1 sprig

Good quality chicken stock 1.2 litres (2 pints)

Roast chicken, skinless 300g (11oz), roughly chopped

Salt and freshly ground black pepper

Seeded bread 1 slice, lightly toasted

Chopped fresh sage 2 tbsp

Heat 1 tablespoon olive oil in a large saucepan and fry the onion for 2–3 minutes until lightly golden. Set aside 2 tablespoons of the fried onion.

Add the celery, leek, potatoes, garlic and rosemary to the pan and fry for 1–2 minutes until softened. Pour in the stock and bring to the boil. Cover and simmer for 10–12 minutes until the potato is soft.

Remove from the heat and discard the rosemary sprig. Using a stick blender, whizz until smooth. Stir in the chopped chicken and season to taste.

In a food processor whizz the toasted bread to chunky crumbs.

Heat a small frying pan with a couple of sprays of olive oil. Add the reserved onion, the breadcrumbs and the sage and fry for 2–3 minutes until crisp and golden. Season to taste and spoon into a small serving bowl.

Ladle the soup into bowls and sprinkle with the sage and onion crumbs.

Tips

This is a great way of using up roast chicken. If you have any leftover veg, chop and stir them in with the chicken.

NOTES

Calories	Fibre	Salt	Sugar	Fat
241	4.6g	1.8g	0g	7.7g of which 1.6g is saturated

TURKEY, HAM & BUTTER BEAN BROTH

Serves 6   Preparation 25 minutes   Cooking 30 minutes

Butter 50g (2oz)

Onion 1, peeled and chopped

Celery 2 sticks, sliced

Leeks 2, trimmed and sliced

Carrots 350g (12oz), peeled and cut into small chunks

Potatoes 250g (9oz), peeled and cut into small chunks

Bay leaves 2, torn

Thyme 2 sprigs, or ½ tsp dried

Chopped fresh rosemary 2 tsp, or ½ tsp dried

Ham or chicken stock 2 litres (3½ pints), hot

Skinless turkey steaks 250g (9oz)

Ham 150g (5oz), trimmed of fat and thickly sliced

Baby spinach 75g (3oz)

Butter beans 2 x 400g cans, rinsed and drained

Chicken gravy granules 3 tbsp

Chopped fresh parsley 25g (1oz)

Salt and freshly ground black pepper

Melt the butter in a large saucepan, add the onion, celery, leeks, carrots and potatoes and stir to coat. Add the bay leaves, thyme and rosemary, pour in the hot stock and bring to the boil.

Add the turkey then reduce the heat and simmer for 15 minutes.

Remove the cooked turkey to a board and shred or slice it. Return to the saucepan with the ham, spinach and butter beans. Stir in the gravy granules and parsley and simmer for 10 minutes. Taste and adjust the seasoning. Serve piping hot.

Tips

Instead of spinach, you could use finely shredded cabbage or torn watercress.

Serve with crusty bread for a crowd-pleasing main-course soup.

Serve each bowlful with 15g (½oz) grated mature Cheddar or Parmesan cheese, sprinkled on just before serving.

NOTES

Calories	Fibre	Salt	Sugar	Fat
272	10.7g	1.4g	0g	9.3g of which 5g is saturated

COUSCOUS SALAD WITH ROASTED VEGETABLES & FETA

Serves 2   Preparation 15 minutes   Cooking 40 minutes

Sweet Ramiro pepper 1, deseeded and roughly chopped

Courgette 1, roughly chopped

Red onion 1, peeled and thickly sliced

Italian herb seasoning 1 tbsp

Olive oil 1 tbsp

Feta cheese 50g (2oz), cut into 2 thin square slices and seasoned with black pepper

Balsamic vinegar 1 tbsp

Salt and freshly ground black pepper

Wholewheat couscous 75g (3oz)

Vegetable stock 125ml (4fl oz), hot

Lentil sprout mix (Good 4 U Salad Topper) 50g (2oz)

Wild rocket 2 handfuls

Preheat the oven to 180°C/160°fan/Gas 4. Put all the vegetables into a small roasting tin and mix in the Italian herb seasoning and 1 tablespoon olive oil. Roast for 20 minutes.

Line a baking tray with non-stick baking paper. Turn the vegetables and place the feta slices on the lined tray on the shelf below. Roast for a further 15 minutes. Add the balsamic vinegar and seasoning to the vegetables and stir through.

Meanwhile, put the couscous in a bowl and pour over the hot stock. Cover the bowl and leave to stand for 5 minutes. Using a fork, fluff up the grains to separate them then stir in the lentil sprout mix. Add the roasted vegetables to the couscous and stir thoroughly to coat the grains in the juices.

Spoon the couscous onto serving plates and top with the feta and a handful of wild rocket.

Tips

Ramiro peppers are sweet pointed peppers, which are perfect for roasting.

Instead of couscous, try this with other grains or pulses, such as quinoa or lentils.

For a vegan version, leave out the feta and pan-fry avocado slices.

NOTES

Calories	Fibre	Salt	Sugar	Fat
351	7.9g	2.3g	0g	14.2g of which 4.8g is saturated

PRETTY PEANUT NOODLE SALAD

Serves 2   Preparation 20 minutes   Cooking 4 minutes

Fine egg noodles 100g (3½oz)

Sesame oil 1 tsp

Smooth peanut butter 25g (1oz)

Light soy sauce 2 tbsp

White balsamic vinegar 1 tbsp

Maple carob syrup 2 tsp

Baby cucumbers 2

Carrot 1, peeled and coarsely grated

Salad cress 1 carton, trimmed

Spring onion 1, trimmed and finely chopped

Radishes 4, trimmed and thinly sliced

Cook the noodles according to the pack's instructions. Drain well and return to the pan.

While the noodles are cooking, whisk the sesame oil, peanut butter, soy sauce, vinegar and syrup together. Mix half the peanut dressing into the drained noodles and leave to cool.

Trim the cucumbers and cut into short thin lengths or shave into strips using a vegetable peeler.

Using two forks, carefully mix the cucumbers, carrots and cress into the noodles. Pile into serving bowls and scatter with spring onion and radishes. Serve with the remaining peanut dressing alongside.

Tips

For a gluten-free version, use rice noodles and gluten-free soy sauce. For a main meal salad, add pieces of cooked chicken or some peeled prawns to the noodles and vegetables. Use ordinary balsamic vinegar if you prefer.

NOTES

Calories	Fibre	Salt	Sugar	Fat
342	6.4g	2.6g	3g	13.7g of which 2.7g is saturated

BEJEWELLED RICE SALAD

Serves 2   Preparation 20 minutes   Cooking 20 minutes

Olive oil spray

Red onion 1 small, peeled and finely chopped

Yellow pepper 1 small, deseeded and chopped

Red chilli 1, deseeded and finely chopped

Medium curry powder 1½ tsp

Bay leaf 1

Salt and freshly ground black pepper

Cauliflower florets 200g (7oz)

Ready-cooked wholegrain rice 250g pack

Baby cucumber 1, chopped

Tomatoes 125g (4½oz), chopped

Chopped fresh coriander 2 tbsp

Pomegranate seeds 2 tbsp

Ready-to-eat plain poppadoms 4

Lightly spray a non-stick frying pan with oil and heat until hot. Add the onion, pepper, chilli, curry powder, bay leaf, salt and pepper and stir-fry for 2 minutes. Cover the pan with a tight-fitting lid, reduce the heat to low and leave the vegetables to cook gently in their own steam, stirring occasionally, for 15 minutes.

Meanwhile, cook the cauliflower in a small saucepan of lightly salted boiling water for 2–3 minutes until slightly softened – do not cook completely. Drain well.

Stir the cauliflower and rice into the spicy vegetables and cook, stirring, for 3–4 minutes until thoroughly heated through. Turn off the heat. Cover and leave to stand for 10 minutes. Discard the bay leaf and season with salt to taste.

To serve, pile the vegetable rice into warmed serving bowls. Mix the cucumber, tomatoes and coriander together and sprinkle on top. Scatter with pomegranate seeds and serve warm accompanied with the poppadoms.

Tips

Take care not to overcook the cauliflower.

Instead of rice, try other cooked grains such as quinoa, spelt or wheatberries. For extra crunch, sprinkle the salad with a few toasted seeds or flaked almonds before serving.

Use chopped mint instead of coriander if preferred.

You can prepare the vegetables for this recipe up to 24 hours in advance and then reheat with the rice, as above, for 5 minutes.

NOTES

Calories	Fibre	Salt	Sugar	Fat
400	11.3g	1.6g	0g	6.3g of which 0.4g is saturated

MEXICAN-INSPIRED CHILLI EGG ROLLS

Serves 2   Preparation 15 minutes   Cooking 6 minutes

Avocado 1

Tomato 1 large

Dried chilli flakes ½ tsp

Fajita seasoning 1 tsp

Eggs 3 medium, beaten

Spring onions 2, trimmed and finely chopped

Sweet chilli sauce 4 tsp, plus extra to serve

Olive oil spray

Wholewheat soft tortillas 2

Coriander leaves handful

Green salad to serve (optional)

Peel and stone the avocado, then mash until smooth. Chop the tomato into small pieces and mix with the avocado along with the chilli flakes and fajita seasoning. Set aside.

Mix together the eggs, spring onions and chilli sauce. Lightly spray a small (20cm/8in) non-stick frying pan with oil and heat until hot. Pour in half the egg mixture. Cook gently for 2 minutes until just set, then turn over and cook for a further minute. Drain and keep warm while you cook the remaining egg mixture in the same way.

Heat the tortillas according to the pack's instructions and spread with the avocado mixture to within 2.5cm (1in) of the edge. Sprinkle with coriander leaves and top with an omelette. Working on one wrap at a time, fold two opposite sides quarter-way towards the centre, then bring the bottom side up towards the centre and continue folding or rolling until you reach the top.

Best eaten warm accompanied with more chilli sauce and a green salad.

Tip

For a high-fibre filling, replace the avocado with mashed, cooked white beans or kidney beans.

NOTES

Calories	Fibre	Salt	Sugar	Fat
463	11.6g	1.6g	5.7g	25.3g of which 6.9g is saturated

GARLICKY MUSHROOMS ON CIABATTA

Serves 2   Preparation 5 minutes   Cooking 15 minutes

Light olive oil 2 tsp

Shallot 1, peeled and chopped

Garlic 1 clove, peeled and chopped

Field mushrooms 200g (7oz), chopped into bite-sized pieces

Baby spinach 125g (4½oz)

Reduced fat soft cheese with garlic and herbs 25g (1oz)

Basil or parsley leaves 25g (1oz), chopped

Salt and freshly ground black pepper

Ciabatta loaf ½

Parmesan-style cheese 25g (1oz), shaved using a vegetable peeler

Heat the olive oil in a large non-stick frying pan or wok, add the shallot and garlic and cook gently for 3–4 minutes until starting to soften.

Add the mushrooms, turn up the heat and stir-fry for 5 minutes. Toss in the spinach and cook until the leaves begin to wilt.

Reduce the heat, add the soft cheese, fresh herbs and a little salt and pepper to taste. Stir through to melt the cheese and lightly coat the mushrooms.

Meanwhile, split the ciabatta horizontally and toast until golden and crunchy. Using a slotted spoon, spoon the spinach and mushroom mixture onto the ciabatta slices.

Increase the heat under the pan and bubble the pan juices to reduce to about 3 tablespoons. Drizzle over the mushrooms and scatter over the Parmesan shavings.

Tips

If cooking for vegetarians, make sure you use a suitable cheese.

Reduced fat soft cheeses are handy to keep in the fridge for that added spoonful of creaminess for pasta, dips and sauces

Serve the mushroom and spinach mix as a side dish for grilled chicken or steaks, accompanied with a green salad, with or without the ciabatta.

The mushroom and spinach mix also makes a substantial filling for an omelette.

NOTES

Calories	Fibre	Salt	Sugar	Fat
356	4g	1.9g	1.9g	18.2g of which 4.7g is saturated

EGGS FLORENTINE

Serves 2   Preparation 10 minutes   Cooking 20 minutes

White wine vinegar 1 tbsp

Eggs 2-4

Baby spinach leaves 225g pack

Leek 1 large, trimmed, washed, halved and finely shredded

Smoked back bacon 4 rashers

Low-fat plain fromage frais 4 tbsp

Ground nutmeg 1¼ tsp

Salt and freshly ground black pepper

Toasted seeded bread buttered, to serve (optional)

Half fill a saucepan with water and add the vinegar. Bring the water to the boil, then reduce to a gentle simmer. Carefully break each egg into a cup and slide into the water. Simmer for 3–5 minutes. Remove from the heat and keep warm in the water until ready to serve.

Meanwhile, rinse the spinach and pack into a saucepan without drying. Add the leek and mix together well. Cover and place over a medium heat for 4–5 minutes until wilted.

Preheat the grill to hot and grill the bacon rashers until cooked, turning once. Cut into slices.

Meanwhile, drain the spinach and leek by pressing the vegetables against the side of a colander or sieve to remove as much liquid as possible, and return to the saucepan. Stir in the fromage frais and nutmeg and add seasoning to taste.

Divide the spinach between two warmed plates and top with the bacon. Drain the eggs using a slotted spoon and place one or two on top of each pile. Dust with extra nutmeg and black pepper and serve with slices of hot buttered toast, if liked.

Tip

Spinach might look bulky when it's fresh, but it wilts and reduces in size very quickly when cooked.

NOTES

Calories	Fibre	Salt	Sugar	Fat
244	3.6g	2.7g	0g	15.5g fat of which 5.2g is saturated

SMOKED MACKEREL & APPLE TOASTIES

Serves 2   Preparation 15 minutes   Cooking 2 minutes

Reduced fat soft cheese 50g (2oz)

Lemon juice 2 tsp

Creamed horseradish sauce 2 tsp

Smoked mackerel fillets 150g (5oz), skinned and flaked

Freshly ground black pepper

Tart dessert apple (such as Granny Smith) 1, cut into quarters and cored

Chopped fresh chives or parsley 2 tsp

Oaty wholemeal bread 4 thick slices

Watercress 25g (1oz)

Beat together the cheese, lemon juice and horseradish. Fold in the mackerel flakes then season well with pepper.

Coarsely grate the apple, discarding the skin. Fold into the mackerel together with the chopped herbs.

Lightly toast the bread. Spread the mackerel mix over two slices, pile on the watercress and top with the remaining slices of toast, pressing firmly. To serve, cut each sandwich in half.

Tips

Mackerel, like other oily fish, is rich in essential omega-3 fats. This fishy mix makes a good toastie or lunchbox sandwich, a filling for a warmed pitta bread, a topping for a jacket potato, or a delicious dip, accompanied with sticks of red or yellow peppers, celery and carrot.

For a more substantial lunch, serve with a winter salad of sliced beetroot, carrot and cucumber.

NOTES

Calories	Fibre	Salt	Sugar	Fat
426	5.6g	2.4g	1.9g	21.4g of which 4.8g is saturated

SHAKSHUKA

Serves 1   Preparation 5 minutes   Cooking 20 minutes

Olive oil spray

Red onion 1 small, peeled and finely chopped

Red chilli 1 small, deseeded and chopped

Garlic 1 clove, peeled and sliced

Ground cumin 1 tsp

Chopped tomatoes 400g can

Salt and freshly ground black pepper

Eggs 2 medium

Coriander leaves handful, roughly chopped

Crusty bread to serve

Heat a non-stick frying pan or wok and spray with olive oil. Add the onion, chilli and garlic and cook gently for 3–4 minutes until starting to soften.

Sprinkle in the cumin, cook for 1 minute then stir in the chopped tomatoes. Increase the heat and leave to simmer for 5–8 minutes until the sauce has reduced and thickened.

Turn the heat down to a gentle simmer. Season the sauce with salt and pepper to taste.

Using the back of a spoon, make two hollows in the sauce and carefully crack in the eggs. Scatter with the coriander and cover the pan with a lid. Cook for 4–5 minutes or until the eggs are set to your liking. Serve with crusty bread.

Tips

Shakshuka is a classic North African and Middle Eastern dish, which is usually eaten for breakfast or brunch but makes an easy meal for any time of the day. You can easily double up the quantities for 2–4 servings but double up on frying pans too.

You can add chopped green pepper when frying the onion, and a pinch of ras el hanout spice mix if you like.

Make up a large batch of the tomato sauce then freeze in individual portions. With eggs in the fridge, you'll always have a nutritious meal at hand.

NOTES

Calories	Fibre	Salt	Sugar	Fat
292	5.7g	1.5g	0g	11.1g of which 2.7g is saturated

SPAGHETTI TORTILLA

Serves 2   Preparation 15 minutes   Cooking 30 minutes

Wholewheat spaghetti 75g (3oz)

Salt and freshly ground black pepper

Olive oil spray

Spring onions 2, trimmed and chopped

Frozen sliced peppers 100g (3½oz)

Button mushrooms 75g (3oz), sliced

Reduced fat soft cheese with garlic and herbs 100g (3½oz)

Eggs 3 medium

Wild rocket 15g (½oz)

Parmesan-style cheese 15g (½oz), grated

Balsamic vinegar glaze or drizzle 1 tbsp

Break the spaghetti into short lengths. Cook in a pan of lightly salted boiling water for 8–10 minutes until just cooked. Drain well.

Meanwhile, spray a small (approx. 20cm/8in) non-stick frying pan with oil and heat until hot. Add the spring onions, frozen peppers and mushrooms and stir-fry for 3–4 minutes until softened.

Beat the soft cheese and eggs together until well blended and season to taste.

Add the spaghetti to the vegetables, pour over the cheese and egg mixture and mix well. Cook over a very low heat for about 15 minutes until set – if you cover the pan with a lid it will help set the egg more evenly.

Loosen the tortilla and slide onto a plate. Put back in the pan the other way up and cook for a further 2–3 minutes to lightly brown the other side.

To serve, slide the tortilla onto a serving plate, pile the rocket on top and sprinkle with the Parmesan. Drizzle with balsamic glaze and serve warm.

Tips

If cooking for vegetarians, make sure you use a suitable cheese.

You can use any pasta you like in this recipe: to make it gluten-free use a non-wheat pasta. It is great for using up leftover vegetables – just chop them and add them to the mix. Use a fresh pepper, if you prefer, also peas, sweetcorn and chopped green beans work particularly well.

NOTES

Calories	Fibre	Salt	Sugar	Fat
321	4.7g	1.7g	4.7g	12.3g of which 4.8g is saturated

PERFECT POTATOES

Serves 4   Preparation 10 minutes   Cooking 1 hour

Baking potatoes 4, scrubbed and pricked with a fork

Reduced fat soft cheese 150g (5oz)

Eggs 2, hard-boiled, shelled and chopped

Canned sweetcorn 75g (3oz)

Snipped fresh chives 2 tbsp

Cheddar cheese 50g (2oz), grated

Mixed salad and cherry tomatoes to serve (optional)

Preheat the oven to 200°C/180°fan/Gas 6. While the oven heats up, cook the potatoes in the microwave for 5–10 minutes. Then bake in the oven for 30–45 minutes until crisp on the outside and soft in the middle.

Leave to stand for 5 minutes. Preheat the grill.

Cut a thin slice horizontally from the top of each potato and scoop out most of the potato into a bowl. Add the soft cheese, eggs, sweetcorn, chives and half the Cheddar, stir to mix, then spoon back into the potato skins.

Place the potatoes in a shallow heatproof dish and sprinkle with the remaining Cheddar. Place under the hot grill until golden brown. Serve hot with salad and cherry tomatoes, if you like.

Tips

Instead of plain soft cheese, try one flavoured with garlic and herbs or crushed peppercorns.

If you don't have a microwave, bake the potatoes in the oven for 1–1½ hours, depending on their size.

NOTES

Calories	Fibre	Salt	Sugar	Fat
315	5.3g	0.6g	0g	8.8g of which 4.5g is saturated

COMFORTING MAIN COURSES

VEGAN MUSHROOM STROGANOFF WITH CAULIFLOWER RICE

Serves 2   Preparation 5 minutes   Cooking 20 minutes   Ⓥ

Olive oil 2 tsp

Mushrooms (field or chestnut) 250g (9oz), sliced or quartered

Leek 1, trimmed and sliced

Garlic 1 clove, peeled and finely sliced

Salt and freshly ground black pepper

Cornflour 1 tsp

Reduced fat coconut milk 200ml (7fl oz)

Dijon mustard 2 tsp

Sweet smoked paprika 1 tsp, plus extra to garnish

Flat-leaf parsley 15g (½oz), chopped, plus extra to garnish

Cauliflower rice 200g pack

Heat the oil in a large non-stick wok or saucepan over a high heat. Add the mushrooms and leek and stir-fry for 2–3 minutes. Add the garlic, salt and pepper, reduce the heat to medium and cook, stirring occasionally, for a further 4–5 minutes until the mushrooms have softened.

Increase the heat for 1–2 minutes to rapidly evaporate off any watery juices if necessary.

Reduce the heat to a simmer. Sprinkle in the cornflour and blend in the coconut milk, mustard and paprika. Cook for 5 minutes, stirring occasionally as the sauce thickens slightly. Stir in the parsley and season to taste.

Meanwhile, cook the cauliflower rice according to the pack's instructions.

Serve the stroganoff alongside the cauliflower rice, garnished with a sprinkling of parsley and paprika.

Tips

Tarragon is a great match for mushrooms: if you have some, use in addition to the parsley.

Cauliflower rice is delicious, but if you prefer, serve with 125g (4½oz) long grain rice, cooked according to the pack's instructions.

NOTES

Calories	Fibre	Salt	Sugar	Fat
205	6.2g	1.3g	0g	15.4g of which 7.5g is saturated

BUTTERNUT SQUASH & SWEETCORN RISOTTO

Serves 4   Preparation 10 minutes   Cooking 30 minutes

Olive oil 1 tbsp

Onion 1 small, peeled and finely chopped

Garlic 2 cloves, peeled and crushed

Butternut squash 275g (10oz), peeled, deseeded and diced

Dried chilli flakes ¼ tsp (optional)

Arborio rice 275g (10oz)

Vegetable stock 1 litre (1¾ pints), hot

Canned sweetcorn ½ x 198g can, drained

Parmesan-style cheese 20g (¾oz), grated

Salt and freshly ground black pepper

Heat the oil in a large saucepan and fry the onion and garlic for about 5 minutes until softened.

Add the butternut squash and chilli flakes, if using, then add the rice and stir for 1 minute.

Add the hot stock, a ladleful at a time, and stir until absorbed before adding more. Continue adding stock in this way until the rice is tender.

Stir in the sweetcorn and cheese with the final ladleful of stock. Season to taste and serve.

Tip

If cooking for vegetarians, make sure you use a suitable cheese.

NOTES

Calories	Fibre	Salt	Sugar	Fat
355	4.4g	1.4g	0g	6g of which 1g is saturated

MAC 'N' CAULI CHEESE

Serves 2   Preparation 15 minutes   Cooking 30–35 minutes

Dried macaroni or penne pasta 100g (3½oz)

Cauliflower ½, broken into florets

Leek 1, trimmed and thickly sliced

Lighter spreadable butter 25g (1oz)

Plain flour 25g (1oz)

Semi-skimmed milk 300ml (½ pint)

Dijon mustard 1 tsp

Lighter extra mature Cheddar cheese 50g (2oz), grated

Salt and freshly ground black pepper

Snipped fresh chives to garnish (optional)

Roasted tomatoes or seasonal greens to serve (optional)

Preheat the oven to 190°C/170°fan/Gas 5.

Bring a large saucepan of lightly salted water to the boil. Add the pasta and cook for 2 minutes, then add the cauliflower and leek and cook for a further 6-8 minutes until the pasta and vegetables are cooked. Drain thoroughly.

Meanwhile, melt the butter in a small saucepan, sprinkle on the flour and cook over a low heat, stirring to form a paste. Gradually blend in the milk, stirring continuously, and bring to the boil as it thickens to a smooth sauce. Remove from the heat, stir in the mustard and the cheese and season to taste.

Tip the cauliflower and pasta into a shallow 900ml (1½ pint) ovenproof dish. Pour over the cheese sauce.

Bake for 20–25 minutes until bubbling and golden brown. Sprinkle with chives, if using, and serve with roasted tomatoes or seasonal greens if you like.

Tips

Replace half the cauliflower with broccoli.

Fold 75g (3oz) chopped ham into the pasta mixture.

Drain a 145g can tuna in brine and flake into the pasta mixture.

Freeze before baking; defrost thoroughly before cooking as above.

NOTES

Calories	Fibre	Salt	Sugar	Fat
483	6.5g	1.9g	0g	16.8g of which 6.4g is saturated

ROASTED GNOCCHI & MUSHROOM SOUP BAKE WITH CRISPY KALE

Serves 4   Preparation 15 minutes   Cooking 30 minutes

Olive oil 1 tbsp, plus spray

Chestnut mushrooms 250g (9oz), sliced

Chopped fresh tarragon 2 tbsp

Condensed cream of mushroom soup 295g can

Skimmed milk 150ml (¼ pint)

Potato gnocchi 400g pack

Leek 1, trimmed and sliced

Salt and freshly ground black pepper

Kale 75g (3oz), trimmed and roughly chopped

Grated Parmesan-style cheese 2 tbsp

Preheat the oven to 180°C/160°fan/Gas 4.

Heat 1 tablespoon olive oil in a large frying pan over a high heat and fry the mushrooms for 5–6 minutes until lightly golden. Add the tarragon and the mushroom soup plus a full soup can of half water/half milk and stir thoroughly. Bring to the boil and simmer for 3–4 minutes.

Cook the gnocchi and leek in a large saucepan of salted boiling water for 2–3 minutes. Drain well and stir into the mushroom sauce. Season to taste.

Transfer the mixture to a 1.5 litre (2½ pint) ovenproof dish and bake for 20 minutes.

Meanwhile, put the kale in a large bowl, spray with a little olive oil and massage into the leaves; season well. Pile the kale over the bake for the last 8–10 minutes of cooking time. Serve immediately, sprinkled with grated cheese.

Tip

If you want to add meat, use condensed cream of chicken soup and add two chopped cooked chicken breasts when you stir in the cooked gnocchi and leek.

If cooking for vegetarians, make sure you use a suitable cheese.

NOTES

Calories	Fibre	Salt	Sugar	Fat
264	6.2g	1.4g	0g	8.4g of which 2.6g is saturated

QUICK QUORN QUESADILLA

Serves 4   Preparation 10 minutes   Cooking 20 minutes

Vegetable oil 1 tbsp

Red onion 1, peeled and chopped

Garlic 1 clove, peeled and finely chopped

Quorn mince 350g pack

Sweet smoked paprika 1 heaped tsp

Cayenne pepper ½ tsp

Vegetable stock cube 1, crumbled

Chopped fresh coriander 4 tbsp

Flour or corn tortillas 4

Cheddar cheese 50g (2oz), grated

Pickled sliced jalapeño peppers 1–2 tbsp (optional)

Avocado, tomato slices and soured cream to serve

Heat the oil in a frying pan and gently fry the onion and garlic until softened. Add the Quorn mince, paprika and cayenne and fry for 5 minutes.

Add the stock cube and 250ml (9fl oz) water, bring to the boil and simmer until most of the stock has reduced. Stir in the coriander then remove the mixture from the pan and set aside to cool slightly.

Wipe the pan clean with kitchen paper. Put a tortilla in the pan and sprinkle with grated cheese. Add a layer of the mince mixture then sprinkle with more cheese and jalapeños, if using. Top with another tortilla and gently fry until golden brown, pressing the top tortilla so that the cheese starts to melt. Flip over and repeat on the other side.

Remove from the pan, cut into quarters and keep warm. Repeat with the remaining tortillas. Serve two quarters per person with sliced avocado, tomatoes and soured cream.

NOTES

Calories	Fibre	Salt	Sugar	Fat
271	8.5g	1.7g	1.1g	11.7g of which 3.6g is saturated

MEAT-FREE SAUSAGE & LENTIL TAGINE

Serves 4   Preparation 25 minutes   Cooking 40 minutes   Ⓥ

Olive oil 1 tbsp

Vegan chorizo-style sausages 1 pack, chopped into chunks

Red onion 1, peeled and diced

Carrot 1 large, peeled and diced

Celery 2 sticks, diced

Ras el hanout 1 tsp

Cherry tomatoes 400g can

Dried green or brown lentils 125g (4½oz), thoroughly washed and drained

Vegetable stock 500ml (18fl oz)

Soft pitted prunes 6, quartered

Salt and freshly ground black pepper

Spinach 250g (9oz)

Pistachio nuts 25g (1oz), finely chopped

Preserved lemon 1, finely diced (optional)

Heat the oil in a flameproof lidded casserole and fry the sausage chunks for 3–4 minutes until golden. Remove from the pan and set aside.

Add the onion, carrot and celery to the pan and fry for 3–4 minutes until softened and lightly golden. Sprinkle in the ras el hanout and stir through. Return the sausages to the pan along with the cherry tomatoes, lentils, stock, prunes, salt and pepper. Bring to the boil then cover and simmer for 25–30 minutes until the lentils are tender and the sauce has thickened.

Add the spinach and stir until wilted through the tagine.

Spoon into warmed bowls and sprinkle over the pistachios and preserved lemon, if using.

Tip

As an extra topping to sprinkle over when serving, look out for dukkah, a crunchy spice mix.

NOTES

Calories	Fibre	Salt	Sugar	Fat
344	10.4g	2.3g	0g	14.4g fat of which 2.7g is saturated

COD WITH A CHEESY SOUFFLÉ TOPPING

Serves 4   Preparation 10 minutes   Cooking 15–20 minutes

Egg whites 4

Parmesan cheese 25g (1oz), grated

Lancashire cheese 110g (4oz), crumbled

Snipped fresh chives 2 tbsp

Salt and freshly ground black pepper

Cod loin pieces or cod fillets 4 (175–200g/6–7oz each)

New potatoes and peas to serve (optional)

Preheat the oven to 200°C/180°fan/Gas 6. Line a baking tray with foil.

Whisk the egg whites until stiff. Gently fold in the cheeses and chives and season with salt and pepper.

Place the fish on the baking tray and pile the cheese mixture on top. Bake for 15–20 minutes until the fish is just cooked and the topping is puffed and golden.

Serve with new potatoes and peas, if you like.

Tip

For dessert, mix the remaining egg yolks with sugar and milk, pour into ramekins, sprinkle with cinnamon and bake in the oven.

NOTES

Calories	Fibre	Salt	Sugar	Fat
286	0.1g	1.6g	0g	12.5g of which 7.5g is saturated

CREAMY DILL & HOT-SMOKED TROUT COURGETTE 'LINGUINE'

Serves 2   Preparation 15 minutes   Cooking 10 minutes

Olive oil 1 tsp

Garlic 1 clove, peeled and chopped

Half fat crème fraîche 75g (3oz)

Lemon 1 small, juice only

Hot smoked trout fillets 125g (4½oz), flaked

Chopped fresh dill 2 tbsp

Salt and freshly ground black pepper

Courgette 1 large (approx. 375g/13oz), spiralised or julienned into thin ribbons

Ground almonds 1 tbsp, toasted

Flaked almonds 1 tbsp, toasted

Dried parsley 1 tsp

Pea shoots 2 handfuls

Heat the olive oil in a large frying pan over a low heat and lightly fry the garlic. Whisk in the crème fraîche, lemon juice and 2–3 tablespoons water until smooth. Heat for 2–3 minutes. Add the fish, dill and seasoning. Keep warm.

Bring a large saucepan of water to the boil, drop in the courgette ribbons and leave to blanch for 1 minute. Drain well.

In a small bowl, mix together the toasted ground and flaked almonds, the dried parsley and plenty of seasoning.

Add the courgette to the creamy fish sauce and gently stir through. Spoon into serving bowls and pile on a handful of pea shoots. Serve with a sprinkling of the toasted almond crumb.

Tip

This recipe is super quick and easy to prepare. If hot smoked trout is unavailable use hot smoked salmon.

NOTES

Calories	Fibre	Salt	Sugar	Fat
322	3.1g	2.4g	0g	22.7g of which 6.4g is saturated

SMOKY FISH PIE WITH CARROT MASH

Serves 2   Preparation 30 minutes plus cooling   Cooking 1 hour 20 minutes

Carrots 225g (8oz), peeled and chopped

Salt and freshly ground black pepper

Potatoes 250g (9oz), peeled and chopped

Light spread 25g (1oz)

Ground nutmeg pinch

Skinless smoked haddock fillets 300g (11oz)

Button mushrooms 50g (2oz), sliced

Skimmed milk 300ml (½ pint)

Frozen peas 75g (3oz)

Frozen sweetcorn 75g (3oz)

Spring onions 4, trimmed and chopped

Cornflour 15g (½oz)

Olive oil spray

Snipped fresh chives 2 tsp

Tomato and chive salad to serve

Put the carrots in a saucepan with a pinch of salt. Cover with water, bring to the boil and cook for 5 minutes. Add the potatoes, bring back to the boil and cook for 8–10 minutes until tender. Drain well, return to the pan, add the spread and mash until smooth. Season to taste with salt, pepper and nutmeg. Leave to cool.

Meanwhile, put the fish and mushrooms in a frying pan and pour over the milk. Bring to the boil, cover and simmer very gently for 5 minutes. Add the peas, sweetcorn and spring onions, bring back to a simmer, cover and cook gently for a further 5 minutes. Leave to cool.

Drain the fish and vegetables, reserving the cooking liquor. Put the fish and veg into a 1 litre (1¾ pint) baking dish, cover and chill until ready to cook.

In a saucepan, blend 3 tablespoons of the cooking liquor with the cornflour until smooth, then gradually stir in the remaining liquor. Season and heat gently, stirring, until the mixture comes to the boil, then cook for 1 minute until thickened. Remove from the heat and leave to cool; lay a piece of greaseproof paper on top of the sauce to prevent a skin forming.

When ready to cook, preheat the oven to 200°C/180°fan/Gas 6. Spoon the sauce over the fish and vegetables, cover with the mash and lightly spray with oil. Place the dish on a baking tray and bake for about 50 minutes until bubbling and lightly golden. Serve immediately, sprinkled with chives, accompanied with a fresh tomato and chive salad.

Tips

For an extra treat, sprinkle with 25g (1oz) grated smoked cheese.

For a vegetarian version, replace the fish with smoked tofu. You won't need to cook this first, but add ½ teaspoon smoked paprika to the cooking milk when you cook the vegetables for extra smoky flavour. Use plant-based milk and spread for vegan cooking.

Calories	Fibre	Salt	Sugar	Fat
481	10.8g	3g	0g	10.9g of which 2.7g is saturated

SMOKED SALMON & CELERIAC FISHCAKES WITH WATERCRESS TARTARE

Serves 4   Preparation 20 minutes   Cooking 30 minutes

Celeriac 300g (11oz), peeled and chopped

Potatoes 450g (1lb), peeled and chopped

Egg 1 small, beaten

Lemon 1, grated zest and juice

Chopped flat-leaf parsley 2 tbsp

Smoked salmon 200g (7oz), roughly chopped

Salt and freshly ground black pepper

Olive oil spray

For the watercress tartare

Watercress 50g (2oz), finely chopped, plus extra to serve

Capers 1 tbsp, chopped

0% fat Greek-style yogurt 2 tbsp

Light mayonnaise 2 tbsp

Put the celeriac and potatoes in a large pan of water and bring to the boil then simmer for 12–15 minutes until tender. Drain in a colander and leave to steam off for a minute or two, then return to the pan and mash together. Stir in the beaten egg, lemon zest (reserving the juice for the watercress tartare) and parsley. Carefully fold in the smoked salmon and plenty of seasoning.

Heat a large non-stick frying pan and lightly spray with olive oil. Drop heaped tablespoons of the mixture into the pan, shaping them into cakes, and fry – in batches – over a medium heat for 3–4 minutes on each side until golden: take care when turning as they are very soft.

To make the watercress tartare, mix all the ingredients together, adding the lemon juice and seasoning to taste. Transfer to a serving dish and serve with the fishcakes, with some extra watercress on the side.

Tip

These fishcakes are not coated in breadcrumbs so they are soft, light and delicate. The mixture can be prepared up to 2 days ahead and stored in the fridge; fry the fishcakes when you are ready to eat.

NOTES

Calories	Fibre	Salt	Sugar	Fat
262	6.7g	2g	0g	10.1g of which 1.8g is saturated

STEAMED TOMATO & CHILLI MUSSELS WITH SKINNY CHIPS

Serves 2   Preparation 20 minutes   Cooking 30 minutes

Charlotte potatoes 350g (12oz), cut into 1cm (½in) wide chips

Olive oil 2 tsp

Dried rosemary 1 tsp

Salt and freshly ground black pepper

Fresh mussels 1kg (2lb 4oz)

Shallot 1 large, finely chopped

Cherry tomatoes 150g (5oz), quartered

Red chilli 1, finely chopped

Dry white wine 100ml (3½fl oz)

Sun-dried tomato paste 2 tsp

Chopped flat-leaf parsley 2 tbsp

Preheat the oven to 180°C/160°fan/Gas 4. In a bowl, toss the potatoes with 1 teaspoon olive oil, the rosemary and seasoning. Spread them out on a baking tray and roast for 30 minutes, turning halfway through, until crisp and golden.

Meanwhile, put the mussels in a colander and wash under cold water, removing any beards, barnacles and broken shells. If the open ones don't close after tapping them, discard them too.

After the chips have been in the oven for 20 minutes, fry the shallot in 1 teaspoon olive oil in a large pan for 1–2 minutes until softened. Stir in the tomatoes, chilli, wine, tomato paste and a grinding of black pepper. Bring to the boil then tip in the mussels and stir through the tomato mixture. Cover with a tight-fitting lid and cook for 4–5 minutes, shaking the pan occasionally until all the mussels have opened.

Spoon the mussels into bowls, sprinkle with the chopped parsley and serve with the chips.

Tips

If you don't have a large pan with a tight-fitting lid, cover the pan with foil to seal as it is important not to allow steam to escape.

Be careful not to add too much salt as the mussels are quite salty.

NOTES

Calories	Fibre	Salt	Sugar	Fat
329	7.7g	3.2g	0g	12.6g of which 2g is saturated

RICH LEMON CHICKEN

Serves 4   Preparation 15 minutes   Cooking 55 minutes

Olive or sunflower oil 1 tbsp

Skinless and boneless chicken thighs 1kg (2¼lb) or 6, cut into chunks

Onion 1, peeled and chopped

Lemon 1, grated zest and juice

Chicken stock 300ml (½ pint)

Fresh thyme sprigs 2, or ½ tsp dried

Salt and freshly ground black pepper

Egg yolks 2

Parsley or chives small bunch, finely chopped

Cooked macaroni or small pasta shapes to serve (optional)

Heat the oil in a large lidded frying pan over a medium-high heat and add the chicken. Fry for about 5 minutes, stirring occasionally, until lightly browned.

Push the chicken to one side of the pan, then add the onion and fry for a further 5 minutes until softened.

Add the lemon zest and juice, then the stock, thyme and a little salt and pepper. Bring to the boil, stirring, then reduce the heat, cover and simmer for 30 minutes, stirring occasionally.

Scoop the chicken out of the pan with a slotted spoon and keep warm. Beat the egg yolks together in a bowl, then gradually beat in the hot stock and onions until smooth. Return the sauce to the pan and cook over a low heat, stirring constantly until it has lightly thickened.

Return the chicken to the pan and stir in the chopped herbs. Remove thyme sprigs and serve with cooked pasta, if using.

Tips

Be careful not to overheat the sauce at the end when thickening with the egg yolks; if it boils, they will curdle. If you are short of time, you may prefer to use 600g (1lb 5oz) of ready-diced chicken thigh meat, chicken breast mini fillets or turkey breast slices.

NOTES

Calories	Fibre	Salt	Sugar	Fat
355	1.8g	1.5g	0g	12.8g fat of which 3.3g is saturated

PESTO CHICKEN WITH ROASTED POTATOES

Serves 4   Preparation 10 minutes   Cooking 45 minutes

Potatoes 800g (1¾lb), peeled and cubed

Olive oil 3 tbsp, plus spray

Walnuts 15g (½oz), chopped

Flat-leaf parsley 50g (2oz), stalks removed

Garlic 1 clove, peeled and chopped

Grated Parmesan cheese 3 tbsp

Salt and freshly ground black pepper

Chicken breasts 4, cut into strips

Half fat crème fraîche 4 tbsp

Watercress to serve (optional)

Preheat the oven to 200°C/180°fan/Gas 6 and put a roasting tin in the oven to heat.

Boil the potatoes for 5 minutes then drain well. Place in the roasting tin and spray with olive oil. Roast for 40 minutes, turning a few times, until golden and cooked through.

Meanwhile, make the pesto. Dry-fry the walnuts in a frying pan until toasted. Place in a food processor with the parsley, garlic and Parmesan and season with salt. Add 3 tablespoons olive oil and 1 tablespoon water and whizz to a chunky textured paste.

Lightly spray the frying pan with olive oil and cook the chicken for about 5 minutes until browned. Add the crème fraîche and 3 tablespoons pesto and simmer for 5 minutes. Add 2 tablespoons more pesto then serve with the roasted potatoes and watercress, if using.

Tip

Keep leftover pesto sauce in the fridge. It can also be stirred through freshly cooked and drained tagliatelle for a speedy meat-free supper.

NOTES

Calories	Fibre	Salt	Sugar	Fat
457	5.1g	0.9g	0g	18g of which 5.5g is saturated

POT-ROASTED CHICKEN WITH APPLES & CIDER

Serves 4-6   Preparation 20 minutes   Cooking 1¾ hours

Light olive oil 1 tbsp

Shallots 350g (12oz), peeled and left whole

Chicken 1 (approx. 1.5kg/3¼lb)

Chicken stock 300ml (½ pint)

Dry cider 300ml (½ pint)

Bay leaves 2

Sage 1 sprig, plus 1 tbsp chopped, or 1 tsp dried

Salt and freshly ground black pepper

Tart dessert apples (such as Granny Smith) 3, peeled, quartered and cored

Potato mashed with parsnip or celeriac, and seasonal greens to serve

Preheat the oven to 180°C/160°fan/Gas 4.

Heat the oil in a large flameproof lidded casserole over a medium heat, add the shallots and cook for 10 minutes, moving them around the pan to colour evenly. Remove with a slotted spoon and set aside.

Put the chicken in the casserole and brown on all sides, turning the chicken every 5 minutes or so.

Add the stock, cider, bay leaves and sage sprig and season well. Bring to a simmer, cover, place the casserole in the oven and cook for 45 minutes.

Add the shallots and apples, cover and return to the oven for 25–30 minutes or until the chicken is cooked through. Lift the chicken onto a serving plate and keep warm.

Transfer the casserole to the hob. Remove and discard the sage sprig. Bring the cooking juices to a steady boil to reduce slightly. Taste and adjust the seasoning and stir in the chopped sage. Using a fork, lightly crush the apples into the sauce.

Strip the meat from the chicken, discarding the skin, and divide between four warmed plates. Add the shallots, spoon on the sauce and serve with mash and seasonal greens.

Tips

If you like, reduce the cooking stock a little further then stir in 150ml (¼ pint) half fat crème fraîche.

If you prefer, use 4 chicken legs instead of a whole chicken for ease of serving or freezing in portions.

To freeze, strip the chicken meat from the bones and pack into a lidded container with the sauce. Defrost thoroughly before reheating in a microwave oven. Serve piping hot.

Calories	Fibre	Salt	Sugar	Fat
451	2.5g	1.3g	0g	15g of which 3.8g is saturated

CHICKEN SAUSAGES WITH LEMON & THYME BUTTER BEAN MASH

Serves 3–4   Preparation 15 minutes   Cooking 15 minutes

Chicken Italia sausages 8

Balsamic glaze 1 tbsp

Olive oil 1 tbsp

Leek 1, trimmed and chopped

Garlic 1 clove, peeled and crushed

Chopped fresh thyme 1 tbsp

Butter beans 2 x 400g cans, rinsed and drained

Chicken stock 200ml (7fl oz)

Lemon 1 small, grated zest

Salt and freshly ground black pepper

Steamed cavolo nero to serve

Preheat the grill to medium. Grill the sausages for 12–14 minutes or according to the pack's instructions, turning occasionally. In the last 2–3 minutes brush them all over with the balsamic glaze.

Meanwhile, heat the olive oil in a saucepan and fry the leek and garlic for 2–3 minutes until softened and just turning brown. Stir in the thyme and butter beans, pour in the stock and bring to the boil then cover and simmer for 8–10 minutes.

Remove from the heat and mash until soft and creamy. Stir in the lemon zest and plenty of salt and pepper.

Serve the grilled sausages with the butter bean mash and steamed cavolo nero.

Tips

This is a healthier alternative to the classic comforting bangers and mash. The recipe can easily be halved to serve 2. Chicken sausages are available fresh or frozen in supermarkets; alternatively use turkey sausages. A lovely addition would be some onion gravy to pour over.

NOTES

Calories	Fibre	Salt	Sugar	Fat
268	11.2g	2.2g	0g	7.8g of which 1.6g is saturated

CHICKEN, LEEK & CHEDDAR CRUMBLE

Serves 2   Preparation 25 minutes   Cooking 30 minutes

Carrot 1 large, peeled and diced

Leeks 2, trimmed and sliced

Olive oil spray

Skinless boneless chicken thighs 175g (6oz), cut into bite-sized chunks

Plain flour 25g (1oz)

Semi-skimmed milk 150ml (¼ pint)

Dijon mustard 2 tsp

Salt and freshly ground black pepper

Peas or green beans to serve

For the crumble

Plain flour 50g (2oz)

Lighter spreadable butter 50g (2oz)

Lighter extra mature Cheddar cheese 25g (1oz), grated

Dried breadcrumbs 25g (1oz)

Porridge oats 2 tbsp

Dried rosemary 1 tsp

Cook the carrot in a saucepan with enough boiling water to cover for 5 minutes then add the leeks and cook for a further 3–4 minutes. Drain thoroughly, reserving 150ml (¼ pint) of the cooking water.

Heat a non-stick saucepan and spray with olive oil. Add the chicken and stir-fry for about 5 minutes until lightly coloured. Sprinkle on the flour and cook for 1 minute then gradually blend in the hot vegetable cooking water and the milk and cook, stirring continuously, until the sauce is smooth and thickened.

Stir in the mustard and season to taste. Fold in the carrots and leeks. Spoon into a shallow 900ml (1½ pint) ovenproof dish.

Preheat the oven to 200°C/180°fan/Gas 6.

To make the crumble, put the flour and light spread in a bowl and work together with a fork or fingertips until crumbly. Stir in the cheese, breadcrumbs, oats and rosemary. Scatter the crumble evenly over the chicken mixture. Bake for 20 minutes or until piping hot and golden. Serve with peas or green beans.

Tips

Replace the chicken with mushrooms and frozen sweetcorn for a vegetarian alternative.

Single serving portions can be frozen in 250ml (9fl oz) ramekin dishes. Freeze before baking. Defrost thoroughly before cooking.

Calories	Fibre	Salt	Sugar	Fat
641	10g	1.8g	0g	28g of which 9.1g is saturated

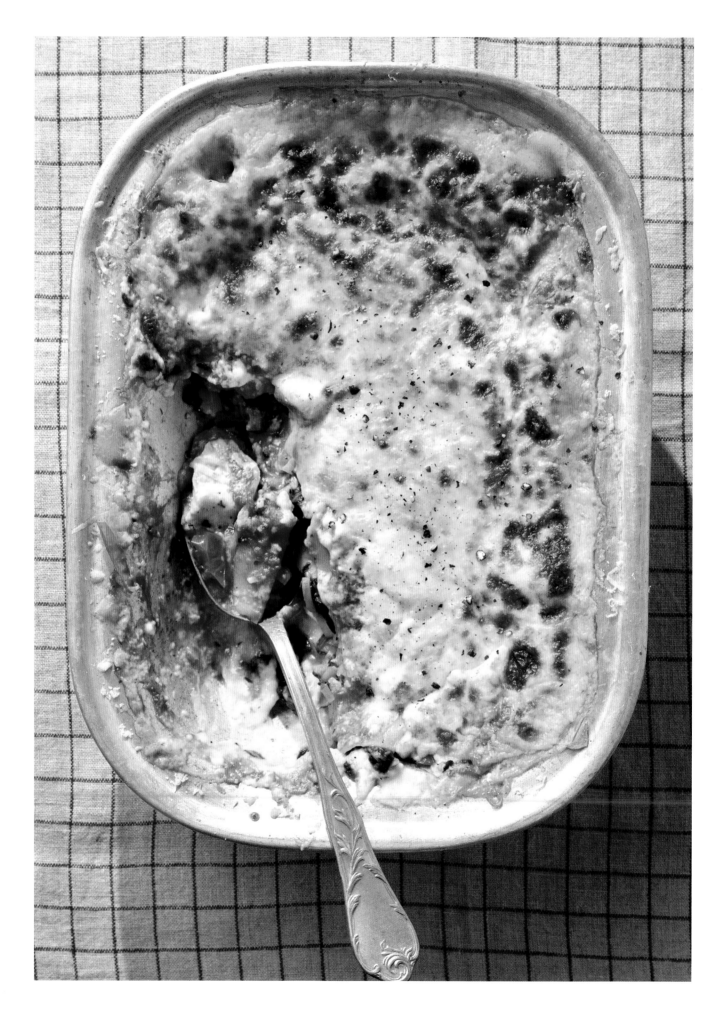

CHICKEN TRICOLORE LASAGNE

Serves 2   Preparation 40 minutes plus cooling and standing   Cooking 1 hour

Baby spinach 200g (7oz), rinsed and drained

Leek 1 small, trimmed and sliced

Salt and freshly ground black pepper

Skimmed milk 500ml (18fl oz)

Cornflour 25g (1oz)

Ground nutmeg pinch

Bay leaf 1

Cherry tomatoes 100g (3½oz), quartered

Passata 150g (5oz)

Sun-dried tomato paste 2 tbsp

Dried oregano ½ tsp

Cooked skinless chicken 150g (5oz), chopped

No pre-cook wholewheat lasagne sheets 4

Parmesan cheese 25g (1oz), grated

Crisp salad and fresh basil leaves to serve

Pack the damp spinach leaves into a large saucepan. Mix in the leek and some salt and pepper. Heat until steam rises, then cover with a lid and cook gently for 5–6 minutes until wilted. Drain well, pressing the spinach against the sides of the colander. Leave to cool.

In a saucepan, blend 4 tablespoons of the milk with the cornflour until smooth, then gradually stir in the remaining milk. Season well and add the nutmeg and bay leaf. Heat gently, stirring, until the mixture comes to the boil, then cook for 1 minute until thickened. Leave to cool; lay a piece of greaseproof paper on top of the sauce to prevent a skin forming. Discard the bay leaf.

Mix together the cherry tomatoes, passata, tomato paste and oregano and season to taste.

When ready to cook, preheat the oven to 200°C/180°fan/Gas 6. Chop the spinach.

Put the chicken into a 1.2 litre (2 pint) oblong baking dish and spoon over one-third of the white sauce. Top with two sheets of lasagne, breaking the pasta to fit the dish if necessary.

Spread the spinach over the pasta and arrange the remaining lasagne sheets on top. Spoon over the tomato mixture and then the remaining white sauce. Sprinkle with grated Parmesan and place the dish on a baking tray. Bake for about 50 minutes until golden brown on top and cooked through.

Leave to stand for 10 minutes before serving with a crisp salad and fresh basil.

Tip

For a vegetarian version, replace the chicken with canned white beans, Quorn pieces or chopped tofu, and use an alternative to Parmesan.

Calories	Fibre	Salt	Sugar	Fat
598	7.9g	1.7g	0g	11g of which 4.3g is saturated

POT-ROAST PORK WITH RED CABBAGE

Serves 6   Preparation 15 minutes   Cooking 2¾ hours

Boneless pork shoulder joint 1.25–1.5kg (about 3½lb), rind removed

Salt and freshly ground black pepper

Vegetable oil 1 tbsp

Red cabbage 450g (1lb), cored and shredded

Dessert apples 225g (8oz), cored and sliced

Plain flour 1 tbsp

Demerara sugar 1 tbsp

Red wine vinegar 3 tbsp

Mashed potato to serve (optional)

Preheat the oven to 190°C/170°fan/Gas 5. Slash the fat side of the pork joint several times and season with salt and pepper. Heat the oil in a frying pan and brown the joint on all sides.

Place the cabbage and apples in a lidded casserole just wide enough to fit the pork. Stir in the flour, sugar, vinegar and seasoning. Place the pork on top, cover and bake for 2–2½ hours until the pork is tender.

Slice the pork and serve with the cabbage and apples, and with mash, if you like.

Tip

For a little extra sweetness, stir in some redcurrant jelly just before serving.

NOTES

Calories	Fibre	Salt	Sugar	Fat
329	2.8g	0.9g	0g	11g of which 3.1g is saturated

HONEY MUSTARD SAUSAGES WITH COLCANNON

Serves 4   Preparation 10 minutes   Cooking 30 minutes

Potatoes 680g (1lb 8oz), peeled and cut into chunks

Leek 1, trimmed and finely sliced

Savoy cabbage 225g (8oz), finely shredded

Lighter spreadable butter 25g (1oz)

Chipolata sausages 12

Milk 6 tbsp

Salt and freshly ground black pepper

Grated nutmeg a pinch

Coarse-grain mustard 1 tbsp

Honey 1 tbsp

Put the potatoes into a saucepan with just enough lightly salted water to cover them. Cover with the lid and bring the water to the boil. Then reduce the heat and simmer for about 15 minutes until the potatoes are tender. Steam the leek and cabbage over the potatoes for the last 5-6 minutes of cooking.

Meanwhile, melt a knob of the butter in a frying pan over a medium heat and cook the sausages, turning them occasionally, for about 10 minutes, until browned all over and almost cooked through.

Drain the potatoes, reserving 6 tbsp of the cooking water. Put the potatoes back in the pan and dry over a low heat for 30 seconds or so. Add the milk, bring it to the boil, take off the heat and add the rest of the butter. Season well with salt and pepper and mash until smooth. Drain the greens well and stir them into the mash with a good sprinkling of nutmeg, to taste.

Drain almost all the fat from the frying pan if necessary. Mix the mustard and honey in a small bowl, then spoon it over the sausages with the reserved cooking water and cook for another minute or so, turning them, until they are cooked through and have a sticky glaze. Serve the mash with the sausages piled on top and drizzled with any extra sticky glaze.

Tips

For fluffy mash you need floury potatoes, so look out for Maris Piper, King Edward and Desiree, or good all-rounders Estima.

Instead of the cabbage and leek you could use carrot, swede or turnip: simply add to the cooking water with the potatoes.

NOTES

Calories	Fibre	Salt	Sugar	Fat
518	9.4g	1.9g	2g	28.5g of which 9.8g is saturated

LAMB & ROSEMARY RAGÙ

Serves 4–6   Preparation 20 minutes   Cooking 50–55 minutes

Lean lamb 450g (1lb), finely diced

Onions 2 large, peeled and diced

Celery 2 sticks, thinly sliced

Carrots 2, peeled and diced

Garlic 2 cloves, peeled and chopped

Rosemary 2 large sprigs, or 1 tbsp dried

Thyme 2 sprigs, or 1 tsp dried

Bay leaves 2, torn

Ground cinnamon ½ tsp

Chopped tomatoes 400g can

Tomato purée 2 tbsp

Lamb stock cube 1, crumbled

Red or white wine 200ml (7fl oz)

Salt and freshly ground black pepper

Dried tagliatelle or penne pasta 350g (12oz)

Parmesan cheese 50g (2oz), grated or shaved

Crisp green salad or steamed green beans to serve

Heat a large non-stick saucepan and when hot add the lamb and brown for 5 minutes, stirring occasionally. Add the onions, celery and carrots and cook until the onions have softened.

Add the garlic, rosemary, thyme, bay leaves and cinnamon. Cover and cook over a low heat for 5 minutes.

Stir in the chopped tomatoes, tomato purée, stock cube, wine and 450ml (¾ pint) hot water. Bring to a steady simmer, partly cover and cook, stirring occasionally, for 30–35 minutes until the sauce has reduced and the lamb is tender. Season to taste.

Meanwhile, cook the pasta in a large pan of lightly salted boiling water for 8–10 minutes or until just tender. Drain thoroughly and stir into the lamb ragù.

Divide the ragù between four or six bowls, sprinkle on the Parmesan and serve immediately, accompanied with a crisp green salad or a bowl of steamed green beans.

Tips

Replace the onions, celery and carrots with a ready-prepared vegetable mix called 'sofrito', available from most supermarkets. This is very handy to keep in the freezer.

Replace the Parmesan with crumbled feta cheese, or replace half the rosemary with a large handful of torn mint or basil leaves, added just before serving.

A ragù is perfect for batch-cooking as it freezes well. Cool the ragù sauce, but don't add the pasta. Freeze in one or two serving portions for up to 3 months. Defrost then gently reheat and continue as above, adding 50g (2oz) dried pasta and 25g (1oz) cheese per person.

Calories	Fibre	Salt	Sugar	Fat
514	8.4g	1.5g	0g	12g fat of which 5.3g is saturated

LIVER WITH BALSAMIC GLAZED SHALLOTS

Serves 4   Preparation 10 minutes   Cooking 20 minutes

Olive or sunflower oil 1 tbsp

Shallots 350g (12oz), peeled, halved if large

Light muscovado (or granulated) sugar 4 tsp

Balsamic vinegar 2 tbsp

Frozen chicken livers 500g (1lb 2oz), defrosted

Lighter spreadable butter 25g (1oz)

Fresh sage leaves small bunch or 1 tsp dried

Closed cup mushrooms 150g (5oz), wiped and sliced

Sherry, red wine or chicken stock 4 tbsp

Salt and freshly ground black pepper

Mash and steamed cabbage to serve (optional)

Heat the oil in a large frying pan over a medium heat and stir-fry the shallots for about 5 minutes until just beginning to soften. Sprinkle with the sugar, add the vinegar and fry for another 5 minutes, turning frequently until caramelised.

Put the chicken livers in a sieve, rinse with cold water then drain well. Tip out on to a chopping board and cut into large chunks, discarding any white cores. Add the butter and sage to the frying pan and when the butter has melted add the livers and mushrooms and fry for 3–4 minutes until the livers are browned but still slightly pink inside.

Stir in the sherry, wine or stock, season lightly with salt and pepper and cook for 1 minute then serve with mashed potato and steamed green cabbage, if using.

Tips

Chicken livers are so cheap and are packed with iron and protein. The secret is to cook them quickly until still slightly pink in the centre. They can also be fried with butter, garlic and mushrooms and tossed with tagliatelle. Or, make as above, adding 2 cloves garlic, then purée and chill until set and serve as pâté.

NOTES

Calories	Fibre	Salt	Sugar	Fat
230	1.9g	0.9g	4.2g	9.7g fat of which 2.2g is saturated

STEAK & ARTICHOKE NOODLES

Serves 2   Preparation 10 minutes   Cooking 20 minutes

Artichoke hearts in oil 5 pieces, halved lengthways, plus 1 tsp oil

Sirloin steak 1 (approx. 150g/5oz), trimmed of fat and thinly sliced

Red onion 1, peeled and sliced

Frozen peas or petits pois 110g (4oz)

Beef stock 300ml (½ pint)

Port 1 tbsp

Soy sauce 1 tbsp

Red chilli 1, finely chopped

Dried oregano ½ tsp

Dried medium egg noodles 2 nests (approx. 110g/4oz)

Wipe a large lidded non-stick frying pan with oil from the artichoke jar and fry the steak over a high heat for 2–3 minutes until browned. Transfer to a plate and set aside.

Add the onion to the pan and fry for 4–5 minutes until softened.

Add the peas or petits pois, stock, port, soy sauce, chilli and oregano to the pan and bring to the boil. Add the noodles, stir, then cover with the lid and simmer for about 4 minutes, until the noodles are tender.

Reduce the heat then add the artichoke halves and the reserved beef and stir for 1–2 minutes, until hot. Serve immediately.

Tips

For extra colour and flavour, fry a sliced red pepper with the onion. If you don't have port, use sherry instead.

NOTES

Calories	Fibre	Salt	Sugar	Fat
433	8.2g	2.9g	1g	11g of which 2.8g is saturated

SLOW-BRAISED OX CHEEKS

Serves 3   Preparation 15 minutes   Cooking 3–4¼ hours

Plain flour 1 tbsp

Salt and freshly ground black pepper

Ox cheeks 2 (approx. 750g/1lb 10oz), trimmed of fat

Olive oil 2 tbsp

Onion 1 large, peeled and finely chopped

Celery 2 sticks, thinly sliced

Garlic 2 cloves, peeled and finely chopped

Beef stock 450ml (¾ pint), hot

Soy sauce 2 tbsp

Maple syrup 1 tbsp

Bay leaves 2

Mashed potatoes and swede, steamed greens to serve (optional)

Preheat the oven to 150°C/130°fan/Gas 2. Season the flour and use to coat the ox cheeks. Heat 1 tablespoon oil in a large frying pan and fry the ox cheeks on both sides for about 3 minutes until browned. Transfer to a casserole.

Add the remaining oil to the frying pan and when hot add the onion, celery and garlic; fry for about 4 minutes. Transfer to the casserole.

Pour the hot stock, soy sauce and maple syrup into the casserole, add the bay leaves and cover with a lid. Cook for 3–4 hours until the meat is very tender.

Remove the casserole from the oven, take out the meat and keep warm. Pour the liquid into a pan, discarding the bay leaves, and boil rapidly for about 5 minutes until reduced to a gravy.

Serve the meat with the gravy, mash and green vegetables, if using.

NOTES

Calories	Fibre	Salt	Sugar	Fat
474	1.8g	4.6g	4g	32g of which 1.1g is saturated

BRAISED BEEF & ROOTS WITH HORSERADISH DUMPLINGS

Serves 4   Preparation 25 minutes   Cooking 2¼ hours

Light olive oil 1 tbsp

Onion 1, peeled and roughly chopped

Celery 2 sticks, sliced

Carrots 2 large, peeled and cut into chunks

Swede ½, peeled and cut into chunks

Lean braising steak 500g (1lb 2oz), cut into chunks

Bay leaves 4

Thyme 4 sprigs, or 1 tsp dried

Plain flour 2 tbsp

Beef stock cube 1

Tomato purée 2 tbsp

Worcestershire sauce 1 tbsp

Salt and freshly ground black pepper

Turnips 2 small, topped and tailed, quartered

Steamed green vegetables to serve

For the dumplings

Self-raising flour 150g (5oz)

Salt pinch

Chopped fresh chives or parsley 1 tbsp

Buttermilk 6 tbsp

Hot horseradish sauce 2 tsp

Preheat the oven to 180°C/160°fan/Gas 4. Heat the oil in a large flameproof lidded casserole, add the onion, celery, carrots and swede, cover and cook for 8–10 minutes, stirring occasionally.

Pat the beef dry with kitchen paper then add to the casserole with the bay leaves and thyme. Sprinkle on the flour and crumble in the stock cube. Mix well then pour in 1 litre (1¾ pints) boiling water or just enough to cover the meat and vegetables. Stir in the tomato purée and Worcestershire sauce and season. Cover and place in the oven to cook for 1 hour.

Stir in the turnips, cover and cook for a further 30 minutes or until the meat is tender.

Meanwhile, make the dumplings. Place the flour, salt and herbs in a bowl. Work in enough buttermilk to form a crumbly dough. Mix in the horseradish sauce and more buttermilk, if needed, to make a smooth, slightly sticky dough.

Remove the casserole from the oven. Taste and adjust the seasoning. Divide the dumpling dough into eight walnut-sized balls and place on top of the stew. Return the casserole to the oven without the lid and cook for 30 minutes until the dumplings are lightly coloured.

Using a slotted spoon, spoon the meat and vegetables into four warmed bowls. Top each with two dumplings and ladle on the sauce. Serve with steamed green vegetables.

Tip

Freeze the cooked meat and vegetables for up to 1 month. Defrost overnight in the fridge. Reheat on the hob or in a preheated oven while you make the dumplings then cook as above.

Calories	Fibre	Salt	Sugar	Fat
452	9.5g	2.5g	0g	11.8g of which 3.8g is saturated

VENISON WITH PRUNES & GARLIC MASH

Serves 2   Preparation 15 minutes   Cooking 20 minutes

Potatoes 450g (1lb), peeled and chopped

Garlic 1 clove, peeled and roughly chopped

Salt and freshly ground black pepper

Reduced fat soft cheese with garlic and herbs 50g (2oz)

Chopped fresh parsley 3 tbsp

Quick-fry venison steaks 2 (approx. 100g/3½oz each)

Olive oil spray

Beef stock 150ml (¼ pint)

Red wine 50ml (2fl oz)

Soft pitted prunes 50g (2oz), chopped

Redcurrant jelly 1 tbsp

Cornflour 2 tsp

Steamed green vegetables to serve

Put the potatoes in a saucepan with the garlic and a pinch of salt. Cover with water, bring to the boil and cook for 8–10 minutes until tender. Drain well, return to the pan and mash until smooth. Stir in the soft cheese and parsley, cover and keep warm.

Season the venison steaks on both sides. Lightly spray a small non-stick frying pan with oil and heat until hot. Add the steaks and seal for a few seconds on each side, then reduce the heat and cook for a further 5 minutes, turning once or twice. Lift the steaks onto a plate, cover loosely and let stand.

Pour the stock and wine into the frying pan, add the prunes and redcurrant jelly and heat, stirring, until the jelly melts. Bring to the boil then simmer for 2 minutes. Blend the cornflour with 1 tablespoon cold water and stir into the sauce. Simmer for 1 minute until thickened.

To serve, pile the mash onto warmed serving plates. Slice the steaks and arrange on the plates then pour over the sauce. Serve immediately, with freshly cooked green vegetables.

Tips

This recipe cooks the venison to medium/rare. If you prefer it more cooked through, cook as above, then slice and add to the thickened sauce and heat through gently for 2–3 minutes. If you prefer not to eat venison, use trimmed lean beef steak instead.

You can cook chicken breast or fillets in the same way, but you will need to flatten the meat first so that it cooks quickly and evenly: lay the skinless fillets between sheets of greaseproof paper and bash with a rolling pin until the meat is about 1cm (½in) thick. Make sure the chicken is cooked through before serving.

Calories	Fibre	Salt	Sugar	Fat
446	6.6g	1.2g	5g	3.5g of which 1.6g is saturated

HOMEMADE TAKE-AWAY

TEX-MEX SKINS & AVOCADO SALSA

Serves 2   Preparation 25 minutes   Cooking 1 hour 35 minutes

Baking potatoes 3 (approx. 200g/7oz each)

Olive oil spray

Salt flakes and freshly ground black pepper

Fajita seasoning ½ tsp

Reduced fat Cheddar cheese 50g (2oz), grated

Avocado 1

Lime 1, juice from ½, the other ½ cut into 4 wedges

Tomato 1 large

Spring onions 2, trimmed and finely chopped

Pickled jalapeño peppers 25g (1oz), drained and chopped

Preheat the oven to 200°C/180°fan/Gas 6. Scrub the potatoes and prick all over with a fork. Bake directly on the oven shelf for about 1 hour, turning halfway through, until tender. Leave to cool for 10 minutes.

Reset the oven to 220°C/200°fan/Gas 7. Line a baking tray with non-stick baking paper.

Cut the potatoes in half lengthways and then in half again, to make four wedges. Carefully slice out the middle portion of cooked potato from each wedge, leaving about 1cm (½in) attached to the skin. Arrange the skins on the baking tray. Lightly spray with oil, season with salt and pepper and dust with the fajita seasoning. Bake for 20 minutes.

Sprinkle with the cheese and return to the oven for 5–10 minutes until the cheese has melted and the potato skins are crisp.

Meanwhile, make the avocado salsa. Peel and stone the avocado, then chop the flesh and mix with the lime juice. Cut the tomato into small pieces and mix with the avocado along with 1 spring onion and the jalapeños. Season to taste. Cover and chill until ready to serve.

To serve, sprinkle the potato skins with the remaining spring onion and serve with the avocado salsa and lime wedges.

Tips

Bake the potatoes up to 2 days in advance. Keep them (whole) in the fridge then prepare as above when ready to serve.

Leftover cooked potato can be used in the recipe on page 116, or to make pie toppings, added to soups to bulk them out or mixed with fish or cooked vegetables to make grilled or baked 'cakes'.

NOTES

Calories	Fibre	Salt	Sugar	Fat
244	4.9g	1.6g	0g	16.3g of which 5g is saturated

BAKED STUFFED MUSHROOM BURGERS

Serves 2 Preparation 15 minutes Cooking 35 minutes

Large flat mushrooms 2 (approx. 100g/3½oz)

Cooked mixed whole grains and rice 50g (2oz)

Parmesan-style cheese 15g (½oz), grated

Salt and freshly ground black pepper

Reduced fat soft cheese with garlic and herbs 25g (1oz)

Wholemeal baps 2 large, split and toasted

Tomato 1 large, sliced

Tomato chutney 2 tbsp

Light mayonnaise 2 tbsp

Wild rocket large handful

Preheat the oven to 200°C/180°fan/Gas 6. Remove and chop the mushroom stalks. Mix the stalks with the rice mix, cheese, salt and pepper. Spread the soft cheese over the inside of the mushrooms and spoon the rice mixture on top.

Sit the mushrooms side by side in a small baking dish. Spoon 4 tablespoons boiling water into the dish (not over the mushrooms), cover with foil and bake for 25 minutes. Uncover and cook for a further 10 minutes until tender and lightly golden.

To serve, line the bottom halves of the baps with tomato. Drain the mushrooms and place on top. Add the chutney and mayonnaise and pile the rocket on top. Cover with the top halves of the baps and serve immediately.

Tips

Small peppers cut in half and deseeded would work instead of mushrooms. Cook the empty halves in boiling water for 5 minutes to soften them before filling and baking as above.

For convenience, use a 250g pouch of cooked mixed grains and rice. Stir-fry the leftovers with onions or spring onions, garlic, ginger and strips of red or yellow peppers, courgettes or carrots; season with soy sauce and sesame oil.

If cooking for vegetarians, make sure you use a suitable cheese.

NOTES

Calories	Fibre	Salt	Sugar	Fat
307	7g	1.7g	4g	12g of which 3.2g is saturated

TARKA DHAL WITH SEEDED CHAPATIS

Serves 4   Preparation 30 minutes   Cooking 1¼ hours

For the chapatis

Seeded wholemeal flour 250g (9oz)

Olive oil 2 tbsp

Salt and freshly ground black pepper

For the dhal

Red split lentils 200g (7oz), rinsed thoroughly

Coconut water (or water) 1 litre (1¾ pints)

Ground turmeric 1 tsp

Garam masala 2 tsp

Bay leaf 1

Coconut or olive oil 2 tsp

Onion 1, peeled and finely sliced

Cinnamon stick 1, snapped in half

Cumin seeds 1 tsp

Garlic 2 cloves, peeled and finely sliced

Root ginger 2cm (¾in) piece, peeled and finely shredded

Green chilli 1, finely sliced

Chickpeas 400g can, rinsed and drained

Chopped fresh coriander 3 tbsp, plus extra leaves to serve

To make the chapatis, mix together the flour, olive oil, ½ teaspoon salt and approx. 125ml (4fl oz) hot water until you have a smooth dough. On a lightly floured surface, knead the dough for 4–5 minutes. Divide into eight balls and leave to rest while you prepare the dhal.

Put the red lentils, coconut water, turmeric, garam masala and bay leaf in a saucepan and bring to the boil. Boil for 10 minutes then reduce the heat, cover and simmer for 35–40 minutes until the lentils are soft and the sauce is thick and soup-like. Top up with extra water if needed.

Heat the coconut or olive oil in a small frying pan and add the onion, cinnamon, cumin, garlic and ginger and fry until golden. Stir in the green chilli and fry for 1–2 minutes. Stir half of this mixture into the cooked lentils. Remove the bay leaf and cinnamon stick, then add the chickpeas, chopped coriander and plenty of salt and pepper. Keep warm.

Roll out each chapati ball to a circle approx.18cm (7in) in diameter. Heat a large frying pan until it starts to smoke. Put one chapati in the pan at a time and cook for 1 minute on each side until it blisters and slightly puffs up.

Serve the hot dhal with the remaining spiced onion mixture, extra coriander leaves and your homemade chapatis on the side.

Tips

The ingredients list looks long, but you will probably have most of the ingredients in your store cupboard; if you haven't got all the spices just use what you have. This dhal keeps well in the fridge for 2–3 days, though you may need to add a little water when reheating.

Calories	Fibre	Salt	Sugar	Fat
520	13.8g	0.8g	0g	11.1g of which 1.5g is saturated

ONE-PAN PIZZA

Serves 2   Preparation 15 minutes   Cooking 30 minutes

Tomatoes 2, halved

Yellow pepper 1, deseeded and cut into chunks

Red onion 1 small, peeled and cut into thick rings

Courgette 1, thickly sliced

Salt and freshly ground black pepper

Light olive oil 1 tsp

Tomato purée 2 tbsp

Reduced fat soft cheese 3 tbsp

Grated mozzarella cheese 50g (2oz)

Basil leaves handful, roughly torn

Balsamic glaze 1 tbsp

Crisp green salad to serve

For the pizza base

Self-raising flour 175g (6oz), plus extra for dusting

Salt ½ tsp

Dried rosemary 1 tsp

Low fat natural yogurt 4 tbsp

Olive oil spray

Preheat the oven to 220°C/200°fan/Gas 7. Line a baking sheet with foil, spread the tomatoes, yellow pepper, onion and courgette over the baking sheet, season well and sprinkle over the oil. Roast for 15 minutes until starting to soften and lightly brown. Set aside.

Meanwhile, make the pizza base. Place the flour, salt, rosemary and yogurt in a bowl, sprinkle over 3 tablespoons cold water and work together to make a soft, sticky dough. Tip onto a lightly floured surface and knead briefly then roll out to a circle to fit a 25–26cm (approx. 10in) frying pan; alternatively you can divide the dough in half and roll out to fit two 20cm (8in) frying pans.

Place the frying pan over a medium heat and spray with a little oil. When the pan is hot, lay the pizza base in the pan and cook for 4–5 minutes until the underside is golden brown. Flip it over and cook for a further 4–5 minutes.

Preheat the grill to hot. Remove the frying pan from the heat. Spread the tomato purée over the pizza base to within 2cm (¾in) of the edge then spread over the soft cheese.

Lightly crush the cooked tomatoes over the base then arrange the remaining roasted vegetables on top. Season well with black pepper then scatter on the mozzarella.

Pop the pan under the grill for 2–3 minutes to melt the cheese. Slide the pizza onto a board, tear over the basil and drizzle with balsamic glaze. Cut into wedges and serve with green salad.

Tips

If you want to make extra pizzas, individually wrap the cooked bases in foil to keep warm before adding the toppings. Alternatively, to freeze, cool then layer between sheets of greaseproof paper and freeze for up to 3 months. Defrost individually, ready to top for a quick pizza supper.

Calories	Fibre	Salt	Sugar	Fat
569	8.1g	2.3g	4.5g	13.8g of which 5.8g is saturated

FISH, CHIPS & MINTED MUSHY PEAS

Serves 2   Preparation 10 minutes   Cooking 40 minutes

Potatoes 2, scrubbed and cut into chunky chips

Salt and freshly ground black pepper

Olive oil spray

Egg 1

Panko breadcrumbs 35g (1¼oz)

Lemon 1, finely grated zest and juice of ½, the remainder cut into wedges

White fish fillets 2 (110–125g/4–4½oz each)

Frozen peas or petits pois 150g (5oz)

Chopped fresh mint 2 tbsp

Preheat the oven to 200°C/180°fan/Gas 6. Line a baking tray with non-stick baking paper.

Put the potato chips into a saucepan and just cover with cold water. Bring to the boil, then simmer for 4 minutes. Drain well, return to the pan to dry off over a low heat for a few seconds, then shake to rough up the edges.

Place the potato chips in a single layer on one half of the baking tray, season and spray with olive oil. Bake for 10 minutes.

Meanwhile, whisk the egg in a shallow bowl. Put the breadcrumbs and lemon zest on a plate and mix in some salt and pepper. Dip each fish fillet in the egg then coat with the breadcrumb mixture. Place on the baking tray next to the chips and spray with oil. Bake for about 20 minutes until the fish is cooked through and the chips have browned.

While the fish is cooking, put the peas in a saucepan and cover with boiling water. Simmer for 4–5 minutes until very tender. Drain well and mash with the lemon juice, mint and a little salt.

Serve the fish and chips with the minted peas and lemon wedges.

Tips

Any white fish works in this recipe. Panko breadcrumbs give a crisp texture, but if you prefer, whizz stale bread in the food processor and use the crumbs instead.

NOTES

Calories	Fibre	Salt	Sugar	Fat
317	5.6g	2g	0g	5g of which 1.1g is saturated

COCONUT PRAWN CURRY

Serves 2   Preparation 10 minutes   Cooking 20 minutes

Light olive oil 2 tsp

Onion 1, finely chopped

Mustard seeds 1 tsp

Red chilli 1 small, deseeded and finely chopped

Ground turmeric ½ tsp

Ground cumin 1 tsp

Ground coriander ½ tsp

Tomatoes 4, chopped

Tamarind paste 1 tbsp

Raw king or extra-large prawns 250g (9oz), defrosted

Reduced fat coconut milk 100ml (3½fl oz)

Salt and freshly ground black pepper

Chopped fresh coriander 2 tbsp to serve

Cooked rice to serve

Heat the oil in a non-stick wok or frying pan, add the onion and cook over a low–medium heat until softened and lightly coloured. Add the mustard seeds, chilli, turmeric, cumin and ground coriander and stir for about a minute until the spices are warmed and becoming fragrant.

Tip the tomatoes and any juices into the pan and simmer for a couple of minutes then stir in the tamarind paste and 6 tablespoons water. Bring to the boil then reduce the heat and simmer for 5 minutes.

Add the prawns and coconut milk and simmer for 5 minutes. Season to taste. Divide between two warmed bowls and sprinkle with the chopped coriander. Serve with rice.

Tips

Tamarind paste adds a sweet and sour flavour. It is readily available in small jars and it keeps well in the fridge once opened.

Swap the prawns for 250g (9oz) skinless salmon fillets, cubed, or 2 small skinless chicken breast fillets, cubed. Add the chicken immediately after the spices are warmed, to allow for longer cooking time.

Coriander stems are full of flavour, so don't discard them when using the leaves for garnishing: chop the stems and freeze in small bags or ice cube trays and add to curries during cooking.

NOTES

Calories	Fibre	Salt	Sugar	Fat
211	3.3g	1.7g	0g	8.3g of which 3.9g is saturated

SHRIMP NOODLES

Serves 2   Preparation 15 minutes plus soaking   Cooking 10 minutes

Dried shiitake mushrooms 25g (1oz)

Dried fine rice noodles (vermicelli) 110g (4oz)

Vegetable oil 2 tsp

Spring onions 4, trimmed and chopped

Frozen peas 110g (4oz)

Cooked peeled shrimps or small prawns 150g (5oz), thawed if frozen

Oyster sauce 4 tbsp

Egg 1 medium, beaten

Salt

Red chilli 1 small, finely chopped

Stir-fried vegetables to serve

Put the mushrooms in a bowl and cover completely with boiling water. Leave to soak for 30 minutes, then drain well and slice thinly. Pat dry with kitchen paper.

Bring a saucepan of water to the boil. Turn off the heat, add the noodles, stir briefly to loosen them and leave to soak for 3 minutes. Drain well and rinse in cold water. Shake well to remove excess water.

Heat 1 teaspoon oil in a large frying pan until hot. Add the mushrooms, spring onions and peas and stir-fry for 3 minutes. Add the shrimps and oyster sauce and the drained noodles and continue to stir-fry for 3 minutes until thoroughly hot. Cover and keep warm.

Season the egg with a little salt. Brush a small non-stick frying pan with the remaining oil, heat until hot then pour in the egg and cook for 1–2 minutes until set; turn and cook the other side. Slide onto a board, roll up tightly and slice thinly.

To serve, pile the noodles into warmed bowls, sprinkle with chopped chilli and top with the egg roll. Serve immediately, with stir-fried vegetables.

Tips

For a gluten-free version, make sure you use gluten-free oyster sauce.

Replace the shrimps with pieces of cooked chicken or lean pork or ham if preferred, or for a vegetarian version, use pieces of Quorn or tofu.

Keep the mushroom soaking liquid for making soups or stock.

NOTES

Calories	Fibre	Salt	Sugar	Fat
337	4.7g	5.2g	6.6g	13.7g of which 1.1g is saturated

CRUNCHY NUT PAD THAI CHICKEN SALAD

Serves 2   Preparation 15 minutes plus soaking   Cooking none

Dried rice noodles 2 nests (approx. 125g/4½oz)

Crunchy peanut butter 2 tsp

Tamarind paste ½ tsp

Light soy sauce 1 tbsp

Fish sauce ½ tsp

Soft brown sugar ½ tsp

Garlic 1 clove, peeled and crushed

Dried chilli flakes pinch

Beansprouts 100g (3½oz)

Spring onions 2, trimmed and finely shredded

Radishes 8, finely sliced

Carrot 1 large, julienned into fine lengths

Cooked skinless chicken breast 150g (5oz), sliced

Salad cress to serve

Roasted peanuts 2 tbsp, chopped

Put the noodles in a large bowl and pour over boiling water, making sure the noodles are completely submerged. Leave to soak for 20 minutes then drain thoroughly.

In a large bowl whisk together the peanut butter, tamarind paste, soy sauce, fish sauce, sugar, garlic, chilli flakes and 2 tablespoons water to make a smooth dressing.

Toss the drained noodles through the dressing with the beansprouts, spring onions, radishes and carrot. Spoon into serving bowls and top with slices of chicken, some snipped salad cress and chopped peanuts.

Tips

This Thai-inspired salad is quick and easy to prepare and healthier than the hot pad Thai take-away dish. It keeps well in the fridge for a couple of days. Swap the chicken for cooked prawns if you prefer.

NOTES

Calories	Fibre	Salt	Sugar	Fat
411	3.6g	1.4g	0g	15.7g of which 3.2g is saturated

PERI PERI POUSSIN WITH SMASHED PEAS & BAKED POTATO MASH

Serves 2   Preparation 40 minutes plus marinating   Cooking 1 hour

Olive oil 1 tbsp

Garlic 2 cloves, peeled and chopped

Red chilli 1, deseeded and chopped

Sweet smoked paprika 1 tsp

Dried oregano 1 tsp

Clear honey 2 tsp

Lime 1, juice only

Salt and freshly ground black pepper

Poussin 1 (approx. 500g/1lb 2oz)

For the baked potato mash

Baking potatoes 2 (approx. 175g/6oz each), scrubbed and pricked with a fork

Skimmed milk 1–2 tbsp

For the smashed minty peas

Frozen peas 150g (5oz)

Dried chilli flakes pinch

Chopped fresh mint 2 tbsp

Using a stick blender or pestle and mortar, whizz together the olive oil, garlic, the red chilli, paprika, oregano, honey, lime juice, salt and pepper until smooth.

Place the poussin breast-side down on a board. Using strong kitchen scissors, cut along each side of the backbone and remove. Turn the poussin over and press flat. Place in a bowl, add the spice mixture and rub it over the bird. Marinate for at least 1 hour or overnight in the fridge.

Preheat the oven to 200°C/180°fan/Gas 6. Place the potatoes on the bottom shelf of the oven. Bake for 1 hour, turning halfway through, until tender, with crisp skins.

After 30 minutes put the poussin in a small roasting tin, place in the oven above the potatoes and roast for 30–35 minutes. Remove them both from the oven and leave the poussin to rest, covered with foil.

Meanwhile, prepare the peas. Cook in a small pan of boiling water for 3–4 minutes. Drain and mash them to a chunky texture. Add the chilli flakes and mint and season with salt and pepper, then transfer to a serving bowl.

Cut the potatoes in half and scoop out the hot flesh into a bowl. Mash and stir in the milk and plenty of salt and pepper until you have a soft mash.

Serve the spatchcocked poussin with the minty peas and mash.

Tips

To check that the poussin is cooked, pierce the thickest part of the leg with a small sharp knife: the juices should run clear (not rosy pink). Use the potato skins in the recipe on page 100.

Calories	Fibre	Salt	Sugar	Fat
566	8.4g	1.3g	3g	26.8g of which 6.5g is saturated

CHICKEN & SWEET POTATO CHIPS

Serves 2 Preparation 30 minutes plus marinating Cooking 30 minutes

Buttermilk 100ml (3½fl oz)

Garlic or celery salt ½ tsp, plus extra for dusting

Freshly ground black pepper

Smoked paprika 1 tsp, plus extra for dusting

Tabasco sauce few drops

Chicken drumsticks 4 (approx. 100g/3½oz each), skin removed

Plain flour 2 tbsp

Egg 1 medium, beaten

Dried white breadcrumbs 40g (1½oz)

Sweet potatoes 350g (12oz), peeled and cut into 1cm (½in) wide chips

Olive oil spray

Reduced fat coleslaw and lemon wedges to serve

Mix the buttermilk, flavoured salt, plenty of black pepper, smoked paprika and Tabasco to taste. Put the chicken in a clean, sealable bag and spoon in the seasoned buttermilk. Mix well, seal and leave in the fridge for at least 4 hours, preferably overnight.

Drain the chicken, then shake off the excess buttermilk but do not rinse. Discard the seasoned buttermilk. Put the flour on one plate, the egg on another and the breadcrumbs on a third. Coat the chicken first in flour, then egg and finally breadcrumbs. Arrange on a lined baking tray and chill until ready to cook.

When ready to cook, remove the chicken from the fridge 15 minutes before cooking. Preheat the oven to 200°C/180°fan/Gas 6.

Line a baking tray with non-stick baking paper. Arrange the sweet potato chips on the lined tray and lightly spray with oil. Season with flavoured salt, pepper and smoked paprika.

Bake the chicken and chips for about 30 minutes, turning occasionally, until tender and cooked through.

To serve, drain the chicken and chips and serve with coleslaw and lemon wedges, if liked.

Tip

Buttermilk is usually made with low fat milk and has a pleasant milky, acidic taste. To make your own, mix 1 teaspoon fresh lemon juice into 100ml (3½fl oz) semi-skimmed milk and leave to stand at room temperature for about 10 minutes until it thickens. Cover and keep in the fridge until ready to use.

NOTES

Calories	Fibre	Salt	Sugar	Fat
544	6.7g	2.5g	0g	11.2g of which 3g is saturated

CHICKEN WINGS WITH CORN ON THE COB & BUTTERMILK MAYO

Serves 4   Preparation 25 minutes plus marinating   Cooking 40–45 minutes

Buttermilk 284ml pot

Chopped fresh rosemary 2 tbsp

Garlic 2 cloves, peeled and crushed

Salt and freshly ground black pepper

Chicken wings approx. 500g (1lb 2oz)

Cornmeal or polenta 50g (2oz)

Self-raising flour 50g (2oz)

Cajun seasoning 2 tbsp

Olive oil spray

Light mayonnaise 2 tbsp

Chopped fresh chives 2 tbsp

Corn cobs 4, cut in half

Finely grated Parmesan cheese 2 tbsp

Put the buttermilk in a large bowl, reserving 2 tablespoons for the mayo. Stir in the rosemary, 1 garlic clove and some salt and pepper. Add the chicken wings and turn them over to coat thoroughly. Chill for at least 2 hours.

Preheat the oven to 220°C/200°fan/Gas 7.

Mix together the cornmeal, flour, Cajun seasoning, salt and pepper in a shallow bowl. Lift the chicken wings out of the marinade, shaking off any excess, then toss in the cornmeal mixture. Place the chicken wings on a rack set over a baking tray. Lightly spray with olive oil and bake for 40–45 minutes until crisp and golden, turning halfway through cooking.

Meanwhile, in a serving bowl mix together the reserved 2 tablespoons buttermilk, the remaining garlic clove, the mayonnaise and chives. Season to taste.

Cook the corn cobs in a pan of boiling water for 3–4 minutes then drain.

Place the corn cobs on a hot griddle pan for 6–7 minutes, turning occasionally until slightly charred. Place on a serving dish and sprinkle over the grated Parmesan. Serve with the chicken wings and buttermilk mayo.

Tip

Serve with a mixed salad to make it more of a main meal. See previous page for buttermilk method.

NOTES

Calories	Fibre	Salt	Sugar	Fat
395	3.3g	1.7g	0g	17g of which 4.5g is saturated

SHAWARMA-STYLE TURKEY MEATBALLS WITH YOGURT DRESSING & POMEGRANATE

Serves 4   Preparation 20 minutes   Cooking 15 minutes

Spring onions 4, finely chopped

Turkey thigh mince 500g (1lb 2oz)

Turkish pepper paste (Belazu) 2 heaped tbsp

Ground cumin 1 tsp

Ground coriander 1 tsp

Chopped fresh coriander 2 tbsp, plus extra to serve

Salt and freshly ground black pepper

Lamb's lettuce 60g (2¼oz)

Red onion 1 small, thinly sliced

Pomegranate seeds 4 tbsp

Flatbreads 4

For the tahini yogurt dressing

0% fat Greek-style yogurt 150g (5oz)

Lemon ½, juice only

Tahini 2 tsp

Chopped fresh mint 2 tbsp, plus extra to serve

In a large bowl mix together the spring onions, turkey mince, Turkish pepper paste, spices, fresh coriander and plenty of seasoning. Divide the mixture into 12 balls and place on a grill rack set over a baking tray.

Preheat the grill to high. Grill the meatballs for 12–15 minutes, turning occasionally, until golden brown.

Meanwhile, make the dressing: stir together the yogurt, lemon juice, tahini and mint and season to taste. Toss together the lamb's lettuce, red onion and pomegranate seeds. Warm the flatbreads in a hot frying pan or grill.

To assemble, place each flatbread on a serving plate, pile the salad and three meatballs on top, scatter over the extra mint leaves and serve the tahini yogurt dressing alongside.

Tips

If you fancy loading more onto your flatbread, add extra salad ingredients such as peppers, cucumber, radishes or pickled green chilli peppers.

Use gochujang paste if you can't find Turkish pepper paste.

NOTES

Calories	Fibre	Salt	Sugar	Fat
514	4g	1.4g	0g	19g of which 4g is saturated

STICKY SOY PORK TENDERLOIN WITH CHINESE SPECIAL FRIED RICE

Serves 4   Preparation 20 minutes   Cooking 40 minutes

Pork fillet 400g (14oz)

Hoisin sauce 3 tbsp

Chinese five spice powder 1 tsp

Wholegrain rice 200g (7oz)

Sesame oil 1 tbsp

Spring onions 4, trimmed and sliced

Garlic 2 cloves, peeled and sliced

Green chilli 1, finely chopped

Root ginger 2cm (¾in) piece, peeled and finely chopped

Red pepper 1, deseeded and chopped

Chestnut mushrooms 100g (3½oz), sliced

Eggs 2, beaten

Dark soy sauce 1 tbsp

Chopped fresh coriander 2 tbsp, plus extra leaves to serve

Preheat the oven to 190°C/170°fan/Gas 5. Place the pork on a small non-stick baking tray. Mix together the hoisin sauce and five spice powder and brush some of this all over the meat. Cover with foil and roast for 35–40 minutes, basting every 10 minutes with more of the hoisin glaze. Remove and set aside to rest.

While the pork is roasting, cook the rice according to the pack's instructions then drain thoroughly.

Heat the sesame oil in a large frying pan and stir-fry the spring onions, garlic, chilli and ginger for 1–2 minutes. Add the red pepper and mushrooms and stir-fry for a further 3–4 minutes.

Push the veg to one side of the pan, pour in the beaten eggs and stir to scramble. Add the cooked rice, soy sauce and chopped coriander and stir well.

Spoon into warmed bowls and serve with slices of sticky pork and a few coriander leaves.

Tips

Replace the pork with cooked prawns: add the hoisin sauce and five spice powder when you stir in the red pepper and mushrooms, then add the prawns to the rice along with a few extra vegetables such as peas, sweetcorn or chopped fine green beans.

NOTES

Calories	Fibre	Salt	Sugar	Fat
414	2.6g	1.5g	5.6g	12.5g of which 3.5g is saturated

BAO BUNS WITH PORK IN BBQ SAUCE

Serves 2   Preparation 50 minutes plus rising and proving   Cooking 40–45 minutes

Plain flour 125g (4½oz), plus extra for dusting

Fast-action dried yeast ½ tsp

Salt large pinch

Baking powder large pinch

Maple carob syrup 1½ tsp

Sunflower oil 1 tbsp

Lean pork fillet 150g (5oz)

Garlic 1 clove, peeled and crushed

Light soy sauce 4 tsp

Tomato ketchup 3 tbsp

Sesame oil ½ tsp

Smoked paprika ½ tsp

Coriander leaves, shredded vegetables and rice wine vinegar to serve

Mix the flour, yeast, salt and baking powder in a bowl. Make a well in the centre and add 1 teaspoon syrup and 1 teaspoon sunflower oil. Add approx. 6 tablespoons warm water and mix to a soft dough. Turn onto a lightly floured surface and knead for about 5 minutes until smooth.

Put the dough in a clean bowl, cover with a clean tea towel and leave in a warm place for about 2 hours until doubled in size.

Re-knead the dough for 1 minute, then divide into four pieces. Form each piece into a neat ball. Put 1 teaspoon sunflower oil in a small dish. Working on one dough ball at a time, on an unfloured work surface, roll into an oval shape about 15 x 8cm (6 x 3½in). Peel away from the surface, brush lightly with oil from the dish and fold loosely in half – do not press down. Transfer to a lightly floured board. When you have shaped all four pieces, cover as above and leave in a warm place for 20–25 minutes until slightly risen and puffed.

Put a steamer over a large pan of boiling water. Arrange the buns, spaced a little apart, in the steamer, cover with the lid and steam for 30–35 minutes until risen and cooked through.

Meanwhile, to make the filling, slice the pork into short, very thin strips. Season with the garlic and 1 teaspoon soy sauce. Mix the remaining soy sauce and maple carob syrup with the ketchup, sesame oil and smoked paprika. Leave aside.

Heat the remaining 1 teaspoon sunflower oil in a non-stick frying pan until hot then add the pork and stir-fry for 5 minutes until cooked through. Add half the sauce and heat for 1 minute.

To serve, open up the warm buns, spoon in the pork mixture, spoon over the remaining sauce and sprinkle with coriander leaves. Serve immediately, with a shredded carrot, cucumber and radish salad sprinkled with chopped spring onions, dressed with white rice vinegar.

Tip

Freeze leftover cooled pork with the sauce for up to 3 months. Defrost and reheat gently in a saucepan until piping hot. Serve with egg fried rice or stir-fried vegetables.

Calories	Fibre	Salt	Sugar	Fat
414	3g	3.8g	5.9g	10.5g of which 2.1g is saturated

KEEMA CURRY

Serves 4   Preparation 10 minutes   Cooking 50 minutes

Onion 1, peeled and chopped

Garlic 2 cloves, peeled and chopped

Root ginger 2.5cm (1in) piece, peeled and grated

5% fat minced beef 500g (1lb 2oz)

Chopped tomatoes 400g can

Ground cumin 2 tsp

Ground turmeric 1 tsp

Garam masala 1 tbsp

Chilli powder ½–1 tsp

Raisins 50g (2oz)

Frozen peas 50g (2oz)

0% fat Greek-style yogurt, fresh mint, basmati rice and naan bread to serve (optional)

Place a large saucepan over a medium–high heat, add the onion, garlic, ginger and the minced beef and fry, stirring often, until the onion has softened and the meat is browned all over.

Pour in the tomatoes with 100ml (3½fl oz) water and all the spices. Cover and simmer gently for 30 minutes.

Add the raisins and frozen peas and cook for a further 15 minutes.

To serve, top with a spoonful of yogurt and some shredded mint, and accompany with basmati rice and naan bread, if you like.

Tip

Minced lamb or minced turkey could be used instead of beef (you'll need to cook turkey mince in a little oil).

NOTES

Calories	Fibre	Salt	Sugar	Fat
249	2.8g	0.8g	0g	5.9g of which 2.6g is saturated

CHEESE BURGERS WITH SLAW & CARROT 'FRIES'

Serves 2   Preparation 10 minutes   Cooking 25–30 minutes

Good quality 5% fat minced beef 200g (7oz)

Tomato purée 2 tbsp

Soy sauce 1½ tbsp

Carrots 2 large, peeled and cut into 1cm (½in) batons

Paprika ½ tsp

Celery salt ½ tsp

Olive oil 1 tbsp

For the slaw

Rice wine vinegar 1 tbsp

Savoy cabbage 25g (1oz), finely shredded

Dessert apple 1, finely chopped

Spring onions 1–2, finely sliced

To serve

Sandwich thins 2

Cheese slices 2

Ketchup, lettuce and gherkin slices (optional)

Using your hands, combine the minced beef with the tomato purée and 1 tablespoon soy sauce, then shape into two burgers. Chill while you prepare the carrots.

Preheat the oven to 200°C/180°fan/Gas 6. Line a baking tray with non-stick baking paper, making a pleat in the centre to prevent the burger juices reaching the carrots.

Add the carrots to a saucepan of boiling water and boil for 4 minutes. Drain well, then return to the pan to dry off. Sprinkle the paprika and celery salt into the pan, add the oil and toss together.

Scatter the carrots on one side of the baking tray and place the burgers on the other side of the pleat. Bake for 12 minutes, then turn the burgers and bake for a further 10 minutes until cooked through.

Meanwhile, make the slaw. In a bowl, whisk together the remaining soy sauce and the rice wine vinegar. Add the cabbage, apple and spring onions and toss everything together.

Put the slaw in two small bowls on serving plates, add the carrot fries and serve each burger on a sandwich thin, topped with a cheese slice and with ketchup, lettuce and gherkin, if you like.

Tip

If you prefer potato fries, parboil the potatoes, drain, shake the pan to rough up the edges and then bake for 30 minutes. Toast the sandwich thins if you like.

Calories	Fibre	Salt	Sugar	Fat
267	7.2g	1.7g	0g	10.5g of which 3.1g is saturated

ASIAN GREENS & BEEF TERIYAKI NOODLES

Serves 2   Preparation 15 minutes   Cooking 10 minutes

Root ginger 2cm (¾in) piece, peeled and grated

Garlic 1 clove, peeled and crushed

Dark soy sauce 2 tbsp

Clear honey 1 tbsp

Mirin (rice wine) 1 tbsp

Dried wholewheat noodles 2 nests (approx. 125g/4½oz)

Sesame oil 1 tbsp

Beef rump or sirloin 200g (7oz), thinly sliced into 1cm (½in) strips

Mangetout 75g (3oz), sliced

Pak choi 2, sliced

Spring onions 4, trimmed and sliced, plus extra to garnish

Toasted sesame seeds 2 tsp

To make the teriyaki sauce, in a small bowl mix together the ginger, garlic, soy sauce, honey and mirin.

Put the noodles in a large bowl, cover with boiling water and set aside for 5 minutes.

Meanwhile, heat a large wok or frying pan over a high heat, add half the sesame oil then add the strips of beef and stir-fry for 2–3 minutes. Transfer to a plate and set aside.

Add the remaining oil and all the vegetables to the hot pan and stir-fry for 1–2 minutes until just tender. Return the beef to the pan and pour in the teriyaki sauce. Drain the noodles and add to the pan, stirring for 1–2 minutes.

Serve in warmed shallow bowls with a sprinkling of toasted sesame seeds and spring onions.

Tips

A simple midweek meal. Everything can be chopped and sliced in the morning, ready to stir-fry later in the day. Alternative green vegetables could be sliced tenderstem broccoli, sugar snaps or fine green beans. Any leftovers can be eaten cold as a salad next day.

NOTES

Calories	Fibre	Salt	Sugar	Fat
511	7.4g	3.1g	7.7g	14.4g of which 3.6g is saturated

BEEF SATAY LIGHT

Serves 2   Preparation 25 minutes plus marinating   Cooking 15 minutes

Sirloin steak 225g (8oz), trimmed of fat

Root ginger 15g (½oz), peeled and grated

Garam masala 1 tsp

Garlic 2 cloves, peeled and crushed

Light soy sauce 4 tsp

Vegetable oil 2 tsp

Creamed coconut 15g (½oz), grated

Smooth peanut butter 1 tbsp

Maple carob syrup 1 tsp

Sesame oil ½ tsp

Dried chilli flakes to taste

Spring onion 1, trimmed and finely chopped

Cooked rice or noodles and salad to serve

Slice the beef into long thin strips (approx. 5mm/¼in wide). Place in a shallow dish. Mix in the ginger, garam masala, half the garlic and half the soy sauce. Cover and leave in the fridge to marinate for at least 2 hours or overnight.

To make the sauce, heat ½ teaspoon vegetable oil in a small saucepan and gently fry the remaining garlic for 2 minutes until softened but not browned. Add the coconut, peanut butter, the remaining soy sauce and 125ml (4fl oz) water. Heat, gently stirring, until melted together, then increase the heat and simmer gently for about 3 minutes, stirring occasionally, until thickened. Remove from the heat and stir in the syrup, sesame oil and chilli flakes to taste. Leave aside until ready to serve.

When ready to cook, thread the beef strips onto four skewers so that each strip forms an S shape. Preheat the grill to hot. Arrange the skewers on the grill rack, brush with a little of the remaining vegetable oil and cook for 3–4 minutes. Turn the skewers, brush with the remaining oil and cook for a further 3–4 minutes until cooked through.

To serve, gently reheat the peanut sauce until hot. Serve the skewers sprinkled with spring onion and extra chilli flakes if liked. Accompany with the peanut sauce, freshly cooked rice or noodles and salad.

Tips

If using wooden skewers, soak them in cold water for 30 minutes before threading on the beef.

In the summer, flash-cook the skewers over hot coals on a barbecue for 3–4 minutes, turning, until cooked through. You can use lean pork fillet or strips of chicken breast instead of beef if preferred – adjust cooking times accordingly.

NOTES

Calories	Fibre	Salt	Sugar	Fat
328	1.3g	1.7g	2g	19.4g of which 6.1g is saturated

INDULGENT DESSERTS & TREATS

BLACKBERRY MERINGUE CHILL

Serves 12   Preparation 10 minutes plus freezing   Cooking none

Blackberries 450g (1lb) fresh or frozen, thawed, plus extra to serve (optional)

Soft brown sugar 50g (2oz)

Whipping cream 300ml (½ pint)

Low fat Greek-style yogurt 300ml (½ pint)

Cocoa powder 2 tbsp, sifted

Meringue nests 4, broken into small pieces

Raspberry compote to serve (optional)

Line the base of a 23cm (9in) springform tin with non-stick baking paper. Tip the berries into a bowl, stir in the sugar and lightly mash the berries with the back of a fork.

In a large bowl, whip the cream until it just holds its shape. Fold in the yogurt and cocoa.

Add the meringue nests and blackberries to the cream, gently folding through to create a marbled mix. Spoon into the lined tin, cover and fast freeze for 6 hours or overnight.

Remove from the freezer to let the dessert soften for 15–20 minutes before serving. Delicious accompanied with fresh berries or a raspberry compote.

Tips

For smaller servings, halve the ingredients and spoon into a lined 900g (2lb) loaf tin or individual ramekins.

Instead of blackberries, use other berries in season or frozen forest fruits or mixed berries.

Ice cream flavours deteriorate quite quickly so use within 2 months of freezing for the best flavour.

Take the dessert out of the freezer and leave at room temperature for 15–20 minutes before serving, or transfer to the fridge 1 hour before serving.

NOTES

Calories	Fibre	Salt	Sugar	Fat
176	1.7g	0g	10.8g	12.7g of which 8.1g is saturated

STRAWBERRY & ELDERFLOWER SPARKLING JELLIES

Serves 6   Preparation 15 minutes plus chilling   Cooking 3 minutes

Strawberries 300g (11oz), plus 3 sliced, to decorate

Elderflower sparkling pressé 750ml bottle, chilled

Caster sugar 1 tbsp, plus 1 tsp

Gelatine leaves 6, snapped in half

Fromage frais 200g (7oz)

Limoncello 2 tbsp

Lemon 1, grated zest

Chop the strawberries and place in six 200ml (7fl oz) serving glasses. Place on a tray and transfer to the freezer to chill for 1 hour.

Pour 300ml (½ pint) of the elderflower pressé into a small saucepan, add 1 tablespoon caster sugar and bring just to the boil, swirling the pan to dissolve the sugar. Immediately take off the heat and leave to cool for 5 minutes.

Meanwhile, put the gelatine in a shallow dish, cover with cold water and leave to soak for 4–5 minutes. Squeeze out the excess water then add the softened gelatine to the elderflower pressé and stir until completely dissolved. Pour into a large measuring jug and top up with the remaining elderflower pressé.

Remove the chilled glasses from the freezer and carefully pour the liquid over the strawberries. Transfer to the fridge to set for a couple of hours or ideally overnight.

Just before serving whisk together the fromage frais, 1 teaspoon caster sugar, limoncello and lemon zest. Spoon on top of the jellies and decorate with a few strawberry slices.

Tips

It is important to keep the dishes chilled to keep the bubbles in the elderflower pressé in the jelly.

If you don't have limoncello you can use 1 teaspoon honey to sweeten the cream.

If you don't have individual glass dishes, use a pretty 1.5 litre (2½ pint) serving dish.

NOTES

Calories	Fibre	Salt	Sugar	Fat
109	1.9g	0.0g	18.0g	0.3g of which 0.1g is saturated

CARAMEL BANANA CHEESECAKES

Serves 2 Preparation 20 minutes plus cooling and setting Cooking none

No added sugar plain granola 50g (2oz)

Butter 15g (½oz), melted

Gelatine leaf 1

Banana 1 ripe

Maple carob syrup 1 tbsp

Caramel flavouring ½ tsp

Reduced fat soft cheese 100g (3½oz)

Fresh fruit, yogurt or cream to serve (optional)

Line the base of two 250ml (9fl oz) ramekins or small dishes with discs of non-stick baking paper. In a food processor, grind the granola to fine crumbs, then mix with the butter and press into the bottom of the dishes. Chill for 30 minutes.

Put the gelatine in a shallow dish, cover with cold water and leave to soak for 5 minutes.

Peel the banana and mash until smooth, then mix with the syrup, flavouring and soft cheese.

Squeeze out the excess water from the gelatine and place in a small dish. Spoon over 2 tablespoons very hot water and stir until dissolved. Leave to cool for 10 minutes then stir into the banana mixture and pour over the granola bases. Chill for at least 2 hours until set.

To serve, carefully run a small knife around the inside of each ramekin and gently ease the cheesecakes out of the ramekins. Serve with yogurt or pouring cream and fresh fruit if liked.

Tips

Leave out the caramel flavouring if preferred and replace with vanilla extract. Or add 2 teaspoons cocoa powder to the mixture for a chocolatey twist.

NOTES

Calories	Fibre	Salt	Sugar	Fat
274	2.4g	0.6g	12.3g	10.3g of which 5.9g is saturated

CREAMY RICE PUDDING WITH PLUM COMPOTE

Serves 4 Preparation 10 minutes Cooking 30 minutes

For the rice pudding

Pudding or arborio rice 100g (3½oz)

Semi-skimmed milk 700ml (1¼ pints)

Vanilla extract 1 tsp

Clear honey 2 tbsp

0% fat Greek-style yogurt 4 tbsp (optional)

For the plum compote

Soft brown sugar 50g (2oz)

Star anise 1

Orange or lemon zest 1 strip

Ripe plums 250g (9oz), quartered and stoned

To make the rice pudding, put the rice, milk and vanilla in a large non-stick saucepan over a low heat. Bring to a gentle simmer, stirring frequently to prevent the rice from sticking. Part cover with a lid and simmer for 25–30 minutes, stirring more often as the rice swells. When tender and creamy, remove from the heat and stir in the honey.

While the rice is cooking, make the compote. Bring 300ml (½ pint) water to the boil in a small saucepan with the sugar, star anise and orange or lemon zest. Add the plums and simmer gently for 15–20 minutes until softened and slightly reduced. Remove from the heat and remove the star anise and citrus zest.

Divide the rice pudding between four bowls and top with the plum compote, adding a spoonful of yogurt, if you like.

Tips

The compote can be made up to 3 days ahead and stored in the fridge until required. It can also be frozen for up to 3 months. Serve warm or chilled.

Replace the plums with any seasonal fruits, such as apples, berries or a mix of fruits.

The rice pudding is not suitable for freezing but is delicious eaten chilled. If you like, serve two portions warm then cool the remaining rice pudding and store in individual glass dishes or small jam jars. Keep in the fridge for up to 2 days.

NOTES

Calories	Fibre	Salt	Sugar	Fat
279	1.7g	0.2g	20.4g	3.5g of which 2.1g is saturated

DATE & PECAN PUDDINGS

Makes 4   Preparation 20 minutes   Cooking 40 minutes

Oil for greasing

Eggs 2

Soft light brown sugar 25g (1oz)

Orange ½, finely grated zest

Self-raising flour 50g (2oz)

Butter 25g (1oz), melted

Dates 50g (2oz), roughly chopped

Sultanas 25g (1oz)

Pecan nuts 25g (1oz), coarsely chopped plus 4 whole

Reduced fat custard or half fat crème fraîche to serve

Preheat the oven to 180°C/160°fan/Gas 4. Lightly oil four 150ml (¼ pint) metal pudding moulds or ramekins and line the bases with discs of non-stick baking paper.

Put the eggs, sugar and orange zest in a heatproof bowl set over a pan of simmering water. Whisk together for 5 minutes or so until pale and thickened and the whisk leaves a trail when lifted from the bowl. Remove the bowl from the heat and whisk until cool.

Sift the flour over the egg mixture and drizzle the butter around the edge then; using a rubber spatula, gently fold into the mixture.

Sprinkle in the dates, sultanas and nuts and gently fold through.

Divide the mixture between the moulds and place them in a small roasting tin. Pour boiling water into the tin to come 2.5cm (1in) up the moulds. Cover lightly with foil and bake for 25–35 minutes until risen and springy to the touch.

Loosen the edges with a knife and invert onto four serving plates. Top each with a pecan nut and serve with reduced fat custard or half fat crème fraîche.

Tips

For a treat, top with a spoonful of Maple Fudge Sauce (see page 153).

For a variation on spotted dick replace the dates and nuts with currants and mixed peel.

These little puds are ideal to batch bake and freeze. Cool completely then wrap individually and freeze for up to 3 months. Defrost in the fridge for about 3 hours and reheat in the microwave oven.

NOTES

Calories	Fibre	Salt	Sugar	Fat
223	1.4g	0.1g	6.3g	12.0g of which 4.3g is saturated

CARROT & GINGER PUDDINGS

Serves 2   Preparation 20 minutes Cooking   30 minutes

Wholemeal plain flour 40g (1½oz)

Ground almonds 25g (1oz)

Baking powder ½ tsp

Butter 25g (1oz)

Semi-skimmed milk 150ml (¼ pint)

Carob fruit or agave syrup 2 tbsp

Carrot 25g (1oz), finely grated

Glacé ginger 20g (¾oz), chopped

Grated creamed coconut 1 tsp

Cornflour 1 tsp

Preheat the oven to 180°C/160°fan/Gas 4. Lightly grease two 175ml (6fl oz) pudding moulds.

In a mixing bowl, stir together the flour, almonds and baking powder, then blend in the butter. Add 2 tablespoons milk, 4 teaspoons syrup, the grated carrot and most of the ginger; mix together well. Divide the mixture between the moulds, smooth the tops and stand the moulds on a baking tray. Bake for about 30 minutes until risen and firm to the touch.

While the puddings are cooking, make the sauce. Put the coconut in a small saucepan with the remaining milk and heat gently, stirring until melted together. Blend the cornflour with 1 tablespoon cold water and stir into the coconut milk. Gradually bring to the boil, stirring, and simmer for 1 minute until thickened. Remove from the heat and stir in the remaining syrup. Leave aside.

To serve, turn out the puddings onto serving plates, top with the remaining ginger and serve with the coconut sauce.

Tips

Try ground ginger, cinnamon or mixed spice as alternative spices.

For a vegan version, use unsweetened plant-based milk and a plant-based spread.

To freeze the puddings, turn them out of the moulds and cool completely. Freeze until solid then wrap individually and freeze for up to 3 months. To reheat, unwrap and invert the frozen puddings back into the pudding moulds and defrost. Place on a baking tray, cover with foil and reheat at 180°C/160°fan/Gas 4 for 15–20 minutes until hot.

Calories	Fibre	Salt	Sugar	Fat
299	2.5g	0.4g	1.5g	19.9g fat of which 8.7g is saturated

LEMON & MAPLE PEAR GRIDDLE CAKES

Serves 2 Preparation 20 minutes Cooking 15 minutes

Self-raising flour 65g (2¼oz)

Baking powder ½ tsp

Lemon 1 small, grated zest and juice, plus extra zest to serve

Butter 15g (½oz), melted

Egg 1 medium, beaten

Semi-skimmed milk 4 tbsp

Maple carob syrup 2 tbsp

Olive oil spray

Firm conference pear 1 large (approx. 250g/9oz), peeled and cored

Natural yogurt or pouring cream to serve (optional)

Sift the flour and baking powder into a bowl. Stir in the lemon zest. Make a well in the centre and add the butter, egg, milk and 1 tablespoon syrup. Stir until evenly mixed.

Lightly spray a large non-stick frying pan with oil and heat until hot. Use a tablespoon to spoon five separate pools of batter into the pan. Cook over a low–medium heat for 2–3 minutes until bubbles appear and the surface sets slightly. Flip over and cook the other side for 1 minute until cooked through. Transfer to a plate, cover and keep warm while you cook the remaining batter in the same way to make 10 small pancakes.

Cut the pear into thin slices and toss with the lemon juice and the remaining syrup. Place in a pan and cook over a low heat, stirring occasionally, for 7–8 minutes until softened.

Serve three pancakes per person with the pear slices, sprinkled with lemon zest. Serve with yogurt or cream if you like. Chill the remaining pancakes and serve with fruit and honey or reduced sugar chocolate spread.

Tips

It is best to choose slightly under-ripe fruit for this recipe so that the slices hold their shape during cooking. Dessert apple can be used instead of pear if preferred.

To freeze the pancakes, cool then wrap and freeze for up to 3 months. To serve cold, defrost at room temperature for 2 hours. Store in the fridge until ready to eat. To reheat, pop in the toaster for a few seconds or in the oven on a baking tray covered with foil at 190°C/170°fan/Gas 5 for 5 minutes.

NOTES

Calories	Fibre	Salt	Sugar	Fat
308	4.7g	1g	6g	10.6g fat of which 5.1g is saturated

APPLE STRUDEL WITH MAPLE FUDGE SAUCE

Serves 8   Preparation 20 minutes   Cooking 40 minutes

Tart dessert apples (such as Granny Smith) 4, halved, peeled, cored and diced

Lemon 1 small, grated zest and juice

Fresh breadcrumbs 4 tbsp

Caster sugar 25g (1oz)

Filo pastry 6 sheets

Sunflower or light olive oil 2 tbsp

Icing sugar 1 tsp

For the maple fudge sauce

Butter 50g (2oz)

Soft light brown sugar 125g (4½oz)

Maple syrup 2 tbsp

Double cream 5 tbsp

Preheat the oven to 180°C/160°fan/Gas 4. Put the apples in a bowl with the lemon zest and juice and toss together. Stir in the breadcrumbs and caster sugar.

Lay three sheets of filo pastry side by side on a clean tea towel, overlapping the longer edges by 5cm (2in). Brush with the oil and then lay the remaining sheets on top and brush with the remaining oil.

Spoon the diced apple along the width leaving a 5cm (2in) border at the bottom and each end of the filling. Use the tea towel to help roll up the pastry from the longest edge, folding the ends in.

Place the strudel on a baking sheet, curving it if needed, and cook for about 40 minutes until the pastry is golden brown and crisp. If the pastry is browning too much toward the end of the cooking time, cover loosely with foil.

Leave to cool on the baking sheet for about 10 minutes before transferring to a serving platter.

Meanwhile, make the sauce. Melt the butter in a small heavy-based saucepan, add the sugar and syrup and stir over a low heat until the sugar has dissolved. Stir in the cream and leave to bubble for a few minutes then remove from the heat to cool slightly.

Dust the strudel with icing sugar and serve in slices, drizzled with the warm fudge sauce.

Tips

Replace one apple with a punnet of raspberries or blueberries.

Add a sprinkling of cinnamon to the apple mix.

The fudge sauce keeps well in the fridge. Store in a lidded jam jar or airtight container.

A whole strudel will freeze well before baking. Wrap in baking paper and freeze in an airtight container. To cook from frozen, add approx. 15 minutes to the original cooking time.

Calories	Fibre	Salt	Sugar	Fat
302	0.9g	0.3g	23.9g	14.0g of which 8.4g is saturated

MIXED BERRY MAPLE GRANOLA CRUMBLE

Serves 4   Preparation 15 minutes   Cooking 35–40 minutes

Mixed berries such as blueberries, raspberries, strawberries 500g (1lb 2oz)

Orange 1, finely grated zest

Maple syrup 3 tbsp

Cornflour 1 tsp

Porridge oats 125g (4½oz)

Pecan nuts 50g (2oz), chopped

Toasted three seed mix 2 tbsp

Ground cinnamon ½ tsp

Butter 50g (2oz), melted

Preheat the oven to 180°C/160°fan/Gas 4.

Put the berries and orange zest in a large ovenproof dish (approx. 1.5 litres/2½ pints). In a small bowl mix together 1 tablespoon maple syrup and the cornflour and pour over the berries, stirring to coat the fruit.

Mix together the oats, pecans, seed mix, cinnamon, melted butter and the remaining maple syrup until you have a lumpy crumble. Sprinkle over the fruit: don't worry about covering the fruit completely.

Bake for 35–40 minutes until the topping is golden and the fruit is beginning to bubble up. Leave to cool slightly before serving.

Tips

This is a healthier version of crumble, with less sugar and fat plus added nuts and seeds. Serve with a dollop of 0% fat Greek or natural Skyr yogurt.

To make this recipe dairy-free, replace the melted butter with coconut oil and serve with a plant-based cream.

NOTES

Calories	Fibre	Salt	Sugar	Fat
394	7.6g	0g	9.1g	23.9g of which 8.0g is saturated

WAFFLEBERRY PIE

Serves 4   Preparation 15 minutes   Cooking 20 minutes

Belgian or American-style waffles 2

Raspberries 275g (10oz)

Half fat crème fraîche 200g (7oz)

Eggs 2, beaten

Vanilla extract ½ tsp

Caster sugar 50g (2oz)

Cornflour 1 tsp

Icing sugar 2 tsp

Cocoa powder 1 tbsp

Preheat the oven to 160°C/140°fan/Gas 3.

Cut the waffles into 2.5cm (1in) squares. Divide the waffles and the raspberries between four 250ml (9fl oz) ramekins or a 1 litre (1¾ pint) ovenproof dish.

Whisk together the crème fraîche, eggs, vanilla, caster sugar and cornflour. Spoon over the raspberry and waffle mix and leave to soak for 10 minutes.

Bake for 20 minutes until puffed up and golden but still slightly moist on the surface. Leave to stand for 10 minutes. Dust with the icing sugar and cocoa and serve warm.

Tips

Vary the berries according to the season: try blueberries or sliced bananas, or mixed berries. Bananas are good with a dusting of ground cinnamon instead of the cocoa.

You can prepare this pudding a few hours in advance. Cover and store in a cool place or the fridge until you are ready to pop it in the oven.

Waffles keep well in the freezer so just take out one or two when you fancy this quick dessert.

NOTES

Calories	Fibre	Salt	Sugar	Fat
241	2.9g	0.2g	16.1g	12.3g of which 7.2g is saturated

BREAD PUDDING

Makes 16 squares   Preparation 25 minutes   Cooking 45–50 minutes

Bread, crust removed 225g (8oz), 2–3 days old, torn into small pieces

Milk 375ml (13fl oz)

Oranges 2, finely grated zest of both, juice of 1

Mixed spice 1 tbsp

Raisins 175g (6oz)

Sultanas 150g (5oz)

Chopped mixed peel 50g (2oz)

Ready-to-eat dried prunes 75g (3oz), chopped

Ready-to-eat dried apricots 75g (3oz), chopped

Glacé cherries 75g (3oz), quartered

Granulated sugar 25g (1oz), plus extra to sprinkle

Eggs 3, beaten

Butter 150g (5oz), melted

Black treacle 1–2 tbsp

Preheat the oven to 180°C/160°fan/Gas 4. Grease a 23cm (9in) square baking dish.

Soak the bread in the milk in a large bowl for 10 minutes.

Add the remaining ingredients and mix well. Transfer to the baking dish, spread evenly and bake for 45–50 minutes until the pudding is lightly browned and set in the centre.

Sprinkle with sugar and serve hot. Or leave to cool, cover and chill. Serve cold, cut into squares.

Tip

Bread pudding is meant to use up leftovers, so if you don't have quite enough of one ingredient, just use what you have in your store cupboard.

NOTES

Calories	Fibre	Salt	Sugar	Fat
227	1.8g	0.3g	3.9g	9.3g of which 5.4g is saturated

SUPER FRUITY CAKES

Makes 8   Preparation 30 minutes plus cooling   Cooking 35 minutes

Pitted Medjool dates 125g (4½oz), chopped
Wholemeal plain flour 75g (3oz)
Baking powder 1 tsp
Ground mixed spice 1 tsp
Ground almonds 40g (1½oz)
Sultanas 100g (3½oz)
Dried cranberries (naturally sweetened/apple juice infused) 75g (3oz)
Soft dried apricots 100g (3½oz), finely chopped
Flaked almonds 15g (½oz) to decorate (optional)

Preheat the oven to 170°C/150°fan/Gas 3. Lightly grease eight muffin tins or line with cake cases. Put the dates in a saucepan with 175ml (6fl oz) water. Bring to the boil, then simmer gently for 4–5 minutes until very soft. Turn off the heat, cover and leave to cool completely. Blitz with a stick blender to make a smooth purée.

Mix the flour, baking powder and spice in a bowl then stir in the ground almonds, sultanas, cranberries and apricots, reserving a few pieces of apricot to decorate if you like. Add the date purée and mix well.

Divide between the tins and smooth the tops. Bake for about 30 minutes until firm to the touch – a cocktail stick inserted into the centre should come out clean. Cool for 10 minutes then turn onto a wire rack to cool completely. For the best flavour and texture, store the cakes in an airtight container overnight.

Just before serving decorate, if you like, with the reserved apricot pieces and flaked almonds.

Tips

Medjool dates are softer than traditional dried dates. If you use the drier dates, cook them for a bit longer to soften them thoroughly before puréeing. The cakes can be stored in an airtight container for 3–4 days, or frozen.

Freeze undecorated for up to 3 months. Defrost at room temperature for about 2 hours.

NOTES

Calories	Fibre	Salt	Sugar	Fat
148	3.1g	0.2g	2.4g	4.2g of which 0.3g is saturated

CHERRY BERRY BITES

Makes 27   Preparation 20 minutes plus chilling and setting   Cooking none

Pitted Medjool dates 200g (7oz), roughly chopped
Dried Morello cherries (no added sugar or oil) 100g (3½oz), roughly chopped
Dried cranberries (naturally sweetened/apple juice infused) 100g (3½oz)
Gluten-free porridge oats 150g (5oz)
Ground almonds 75g (3oz)
Berry fruit flavouring a few drops (optional)
Dark chocolate 25g (1oz)
Freeze-dried raspberry sprinkles 2 tbsp

Line an 18cm (7in) square cake tin with non-stick baking paper.

Put the dates, cherries and cranberries in a blender or food processor and add 2 tablespoons cold water. Pulse the mixture a few times then blitz in short bursts for a few seconds at a time until the mixture begins to clump together. Add the oats, almonds and flavouring if using, and continue to blitz the mixture until well combined.

Transfer to the lined tin and press firmly with the back of a spoon to cover the base in an even, well-compacted layer. Chill for 2 hours to firm up.

Invert a board over the tin and turn both over so the fruit mixture drops out of the tin. Peel off the lining paper then carefully turn the mixture right-side-up. Use a sharp knife to slice the square into nine strips and then cut each strip into three. Arrange the pieces on a board lined with non-stick baking paper.

Melt the chocolate in a small heatproof bowl over a saucepan of barely simmering water. Cool for 5 minutes then, using a teaspoon, drizzle a small amount of chocolate over each bar. Sprinkle with freeze-dried raspberry pieces before the chocolate sets. Leave to set completely before serving.

Tips

Store the bars in an airtight container in the fridge for up to 2 weeks or freeze them undecorated; defrost at room temperature for about 2 hours.

You can experiment with different combinations of fruit and nuts; choose naturally dried fruit without any added sugar or oil if possible.

NOTES

Calories	Fibre	Salt	Sugar	Fat
65	1.1g	0g	5.6g	2.3g of which ?0.4g is saturated

WHITE CHOCOLATE & RASPBERRY CASHEW BITES

Makes 16   Preparation 15 minutes plus chilling   Cooking none

White chocolate 150g (5oz), broken into pieces
Cashew nut butter 2 tbsp
Clear honey 1 tbsp
Puffed brown rice 75g (3oz)
Cashew nuts 25g (1oz), finely chopped
Gently baked raspberries (Urban Fruit) 30g pack, finely chopped

Lightly oil an 18cm (7in) square cake tin.

Put the chocolate into a small heatproof bowl and place over a saucepan of barely simmering water until melted. Stir in the cashew butter and honey and mix well.

Take off the heat and stir in the puffed rice, cashew nuts and raspberries. Spoon into the prepared tin and spread evenly using the back of a spoon.

Leave in the fridge to set for at least a couple of hours before cutting into 16 squares.

Tips

These are perfect to keep in the fridge for when you or the children just want a little something sweet. Try different chocolates, nut butters, nuts or dried fruits. For extra colour, sprinkle with some freeze-dried raspberries before setting.

NOTES

Calories	Fibre	Salt	Sugar	Fat
91	0.6g	0g	6.7g	4.8g of which 2.1g is saturated

BERRY NICE JAM TARTS

Makes 12   Preparation 35 minutes plus cooling   Cooking 50 minutes

Cooked beetroot in natural juice 100g (3½oz)

Frozen berries 200g (7oz)

Granulated sugar 40g (1½oz)

Vanilla extract 1 tsp (optional)

Ready-rolled reduced fat puff pastry 375g pack

Egg 1 medium, beaten, to glaze

Icing sugar ½ tsp

Roughly chop the beetroot and place in a blender with 1 tablespoon of the packing juices or water. Blend until completely smooth.

Put the berries in a saucepan and cook gently until steaming. Cover with a lid, reduce the heat and cook for about 15 minutes until the berries are soft. Lightly mash the berries, add the beetroot purée and stir in the sugar until dissolved. Turn up the heat and simmer the mixture, stirring occasionally, for about 10 minutes until pulpy. Leave to cool completely. Stir in the vanilla if using.

Preheat the oven to 200°C/180°fan/Gas 6. Unroll the pastry. Using an 8cm (3½in) fluted or plain round cutter, stamp out 12 circles as close to the pastry edge and to each other as possible. From the remaining pastry, cut out small hearts, flowers, stars, etc. Gather up the trimmings (see tip), roll out and cut out more shapes to make 12 in total.

Line 12 non-stick tart tins with the pastry circles and spoon in the fruit filling. Brush the pastry edges with egg and bake for about 10 minutes, then add the pastry shapes to the tarts, brush with egg and bake the tarts for a further 10–15 minutes until puffed and golden.

Leave the tarts in the tins to cool for 10 minutes before removing. Dust with the icing sugar and serve warm or cold.

Tips

The best way to re-roll puff pastry trimmings is to lay the pieces of pastry on top of each other rather than scrunch them up in a ball. This retains some of the pastry layers, although the rise won't be as even. Any small pieces of leftover pastry can be glazed and baked as above and used as croutons for soups or salads.

The tarts will be dairy-free if you use plant-based (vegan) pastry.

Calories	Fibre	Salt	Sugar	Fat
148	1.7g	0.3g	4.3g	8.6g of which 4.0g is saturated

CHOCOLATE TRUFFLE BROWNIES

Makes 16   Preparation 20 minutes   Cooking 35–40 minutes

Oil for greasing

Butternut squash 350g (12oz), peeled, deseeded and cut into 2cm (¾in) dice

Dark chocolate 100g (3½oz), broken into small pieces

Eggs 4

Caster sugar 200g (7oz)

Cocoa powder 100g (3½oz)

Plain flour 2 tbsp

Baking powder 2 tsp

Preheat the oven to 180°C/160°fan/Gas 4. Lightly oil a 20cm (8in) square cake tin and line with non-stick baking paper.

Put the butternut squash in a heatproof bowl with a splash of water. Cover and microwave on high for 8–10 minutes until the squash has the texture of softened butter. Drain away any liquid and stir in the chocolate. The residual heat will melt the chocolate. Using a stick blender, blitz to a purée and set aside.

Crack the eggs into a large bowl, add the sugar and using an electric mixer, whisk until light and mousse-like. Sift in the cocoa powder, flour and baking powder and gently fold through.

Fold in the chocolate squash purée. Transfer to the prepared tin and bake for 30–35 minutes until the brownies have set and are springy to the touch.

Leave to cool in the tin before cutting into squares. Serve warm as a dessert or enjoy as an afternoon chocolate fix.

Tips

Store the cut brownies in a lidded container. They will keep for 2–3 days but can become quite moist so freshen up by popping in a warm oven for 10 minutes.

Fold some fresh raspberries into the mixture with the purée and serve as a warm pudding – delicious with vanilla ice cream, raspberry sorbet or a low fat thick yogurt.

Open freeze before storing in an airtight container in the freezer. Defrost and refresh in a warm oven for 10 minutes.

NOTES

Calories	Fibre	Salt	Sugar	Fat
134	1.8g	0.1g	18.0g	4.3g of which 2.2g is saturated

CANDIED ORANGE & PISTACHIO CHOC-DIPPED BISCOTTI

Makes 16 biscotti   Preparation 20 minutes plus cooling   Cooking 30–35 minutes

Plain flour 150g (5oz), plus extra for dusting

Baking powder ½ tsp

Butter 50g (2oz), chilled and diced

Golden caster sugar 50g (2oz)

Italian mixed peel 75g (3oz)

Pistachio nuts 75g (3oz), roughly chopped

Orange blossom water 1 tbsp

Egg white 1

Dark chocolate 50g (2oz), melted

Preheat the oven to 180°C/160°fan/Gas 4. Line a baking sheet with non-stick baking paper.

Sift the flour and baking powder into a bowl and rub in the butter to form fine crumbs. Stir in the sugar, mixed peel and pistachios. Make a well in the centre and pour in the orange blossom water and egg white. Using your hands, bring together to form a soft dough.

Turn out onto a lightly floured surface and shape into a long sausage approx. 4cm (1½in) wide and 35cm (14in) long, squeezing to get rid of any cracks. Place on the lined baking sheet and bake for 20–25 minutes until lightly golden.

Leave to cool for 10 minutes. Transfer to a chopping board and, using a serrated knife, carefully slice at an angle to make 16 slices, 1cm (½in) thick, discarding the end pieces. Lay the biscotti back on the baking sheet and bake for a further 10–12 minutes until lightly golden. Leave to cool completely on a wire rack.

Dip the ends of each biscotti in the melted chocolate and leave to set.

Tips

These biscuits are perfect to dunk into your favourite hot drink or as an after dinner treat. Experiment with different dried fruits and nuts such as dried cherries, apricots or almonds, and almond extract instead of the orange blossom water.

NOTES

Calories	Fibre	Salt	Sugar	Fat
130	1.0g	0.2g	5.6g	6.5g of which 2.6g is saturated

INDEX

THANKS TO

Commissioning/Managing Editor	Emily Davenport
Marketing Executive	Katy Hackforth
Designer	Graham Meigh
Editor	Maggie Ramsay
Recipe Writers	Kathryn Hawkins, Clare Lewis, Wendy Veale
Photographer	Steve Lee
Food Stylist	Sian Davies
Props Stylist	Agathe Gits
Recipe Testers	Lucy Goodman, Hannah Nadin, Laura Pickering, Emma Snow, Gudrun Waskett
Nutritional Consultant	Paul Mcardle
Proof Reader	Aune Butt
Indexer	Ruth Ellis
Market Research	Penny Meigh, Step Beyond
Production	Siobhan Hennessey

Published by Eaglemoss Ltd.
Barn 3, Somerford Business Court
Somerford, Congleton
Cheshire , CW12 4SN

www.dairydiary.co.uk

MIX
Paper from responsible sources
FSC® C020056

Printed May 2022
© Eaglemoss Ltd.
ISBN 9781911388432

Whilst every care has been taken in compiling the information in this book, the publishers cannot accept responsibility for any errors, inadvertent or not, that may be found or may occur at some time in the future owing to changes in legislation or for any other reason.